The Complete Diabetic Diet After 50

Low-Sugar and Low-Carbs Recipes with 21-Day Meal Plan for People Over 50 to Live a Healthy Lifestyle

By Eric Baker

Table of Content

Introduction

According to several estimates, one in ten Americans, or more than 37 million people in the United States, have diabetes, and 90 to 95 per cent of them have type 2 diabetes. The majority of individuals with type 2 diabetes are over the age of 50. So if you are entering into this age group or have already turned 50, then getting concerned is only natural. The chances of developing type 2 diabetes get higher with age, but luckily, there are some lifestyle changes and precautionary measures that you can take to manage your diabetes and prevent its harmful effect on the mind and body. Besides medicinal therapies, diabetic friendly diet and an active lifestyle are the two most valuable recommendations that all health experts suggest to counter type 2 diabetes. There are various ingredients that can be avoided to keep the blood glucose and insulin levels managed. A diabetic-friendly diet can play a major role in fighting all the diabetes risk factors and preventing the progression of the disease. This diet comes with various other benefits, and I will discuss them all in this all-in-one guide on the Diabetic diet for people after 50. You can pick and choose your next meal from the extensive sugar-free, low-glycemic and diabetes-friendly recipe collection and create a menu of your own. This diet can really help you bring discipline into your eating habits, so let's get started!

Background of the Mediterranean Diet

A significant risk factor for type 2 diabetes is age. You are more prone to become diabetic as you become older. Type 2 diabetes is brought on by a combination of your genes and lifestyle. Other factors that can cause type 2 are being overweight, having high blood pressure, and not exercising. Diabetes might go undiagnosed for years for some people. It's possible for symptoms like thirst, frequent urination, fuzzy vision, and tingling in the hands and feet to develop gradually without your knowledge. Diabetes diagnoses really begin to rise during middle age. The higher rate of type 2 development in people over 50 is because of the fact that with ageing, the metabolic processes slow down, the cells go weaker, and the body does not

respond well to insulin production. The damage that prediabetes may cause in adults over 50 is difficult to stop or prevent, and it eventually leads to type 2 diabetes.

The Diabetic-Friendly Diet for People over 50

A smart diabetic diet is very similar to a healthy eating approach that most doctors advise for everyone and it lets you consume lean protein, healthy fats, fiber-rich fruits and vegetables, minimally processed foods, and a limit on refined grains and added sugars. No matter you're your age, if you start eating a diabetic-friendly diet, you can actively reduce the risks of heart diseases, high blood cholesterol and obesity. If you have prediabetes or type 2 diabetes, then a change in your daily diet can significantly help in managing the condition. In type 2, the normal production of insulin is affected, and the blood glucose level rises, which needs to be controlled. You can do so by managing the intake of macronutrients. Here is how the dietary changes can help counter diabetes:

- Carbohydrates and diabetes

Your body needs glucose, which is created when carbohydrates are digested, to produce energy. The largest influence on blood glucose levels is the number of carbohydrates in your meal. You can maintain your energy levels without significantly raising your blood glucose levels by eating regular meals and distributing your portions of carbohydrate-rich foods throughout the day. You might also need to eat between meals if you use insulin or diabetes medication. With a controlled intake of carbohydrates, your body won't suffer from a blood glucose spike, which is dangerous for diabetics who don't have enough insulin in the body to metabolize excessive glucose.

- Sugar intake and diabetes

Those who have diabetes and maintain a healthy eating regimen can consume a small amount of sugar. However, it is not the table sugar I am talking about; it is the sugar or saccharides that are present in fruits and honey. And those too should be consumed along with a healthy diet. For instance, tinned fruit in natural juice, some high-fiber breakfast cereals with dried fruit, natural muesli, and one teaspoon of honey with plain porridge. Other sweeteners like white or brown sugar, maple or agave syrup that contain refined glucose have to be avoided to prevent a spike in blood glucose levels.

- Fat consumption and diabetes

All fats contain a lot of energy. Eating too much fat can result in weight gain, which can make it harder to control your blood sugar levels and your blood fat levels- cholesterol and triglycerides. It matters a lot what kind of fat you consume. Reduce your intake of saturated fat and replace it with healthier unsaturated fats because people with diabetes are more likely to develop heart disease.

- **Protein consumption and diabetes**

Protein is used by the body for repair and growth. The majority of people only need two to three small servings of meat or other protein-rich foods each day. The majority of protein-rich diets have minimal effects on blood sugar levels. So as long as the protein source is free from saturated fats, it is healthy to consume.

Benefits of the Diabetic Diet

The main objective of managing diabetes is to get your blood sugar as close to normal as you can. Your doctor can assist you in establishing your blood sugar goals, but generally speaking, the blood glucose level should be lesser than 180 mg/d two hours after a meal and between 90 and 130 mg/d before meals. Blood sugar is impacted by the carbs you consume. A diabetic diet enables you to better regulate your blood sugar levels by limiting the number of carbs you consume each day and at each meal. Your risk of complications from diabetes may be decreased by maintaining good blood sugar control.

In general, the diabetic diet is a nutritious one. The diet promotes a diverse eating approach that includes items from all the food groups, with a focus on fruits, vegetables, whole grains, lean protein sources, and low-fat dairy. The diet also promotes meal frequency and portion control. These healthy eating guidelines are similar to those offered to someone trying to lose weight. Losing even 10 pounds can be achieved if you have diabetes and you are overweight or obese.

Role of Glycemic Index

The glycemic index divides foods that contain carbohydrates into groups based on how likely they are to cause an increase in blood sugar. When compared to foods with a lower value, foods with a high glycemic index are likely to cause your blood sugar to rise more quickly. The glycemic index (GI) indicates how quickly, moderately, or slowly a diet containing carbohydrates affects blood glucose levels. This implies that it may be helpful for you to control your diabetes.

Foods high in carbohydrates release glucose into the circulation at varying rates. Low glycemic index (GI) foods are those that raise blood sugar levels more gradually and can be beneficial for controlling blood sugar levels. Some high-fiber bread and cereals (particularly grainy bread and oats), pasta, basmati or low GI rice, quinoa, barley, most fruits, legumes, and low-fat dairy products are examples of healthy carbohydrate foods.

Per meal, try to include at least one item with a low GI. When consuming low GI foods, portion control is still crucial because big quantities of these foods can raise blood sugar levels and cause weight gain. Some low GI foods, like ice cream and Chocolate, may be high in added sugar, saturated fat, and energy. When purchasing packaged foods, always check the ingredients list and the energy (calorie or kilojoule) content. Low GI food items have a GI of 55 or below. It is recommended for diabetics to self-monitor their blood glucose levels before and two hours after a meal to see how different foods affect their own blood glucose levels and then manage their intake accordingly.

What Makes a Diabetic Diet?

A diabetic diet does not cross any particular food group of your diet; it simply suggests including more healthy ingredients and less simple carbs and saturated fats. By keeping this one simple formula in mind, a dieter can maintain his body weight, blood glucose and insulin levels. Here is what you can have on this diet:

Healthy carbohydrates:

During digestion, simple carbohydrates and starches break down into blood glucose which is a great problem If your body cannot produce enough insulin to control it. That is why a diabetic person must focus on consuming complex healthy carbohydrates, which are found in:

- Low and medium glycemic fruits
- Whole grains
- Non-starchy vegetables
- Legumes
- Low-fat dairy products

Fiber-rich foods:

Dietary fiber is present in different plant-based foods. Fiber intake helps your body in digestion and in controlling blood sugar levels. Such food items are:

- Vegetables
- Fruits
- Nuts
- Legumes
- Whole grains

Omega-3:

Eating heart-healthy fish at least twice a week is important. Fish like mackerel, salmon, tuna and sardines are rich in omega-3 fatty acids and are good at preventing heart disease. But make sure to avoid eating fried fish and fish with high levels of mercury.

Healthy fats:

All the monounsaturated and polyunsaturated fats are termed as healthy fats and contain high-density lipoproteins, which can help lower your blood cholesterol levels. Such fats are found in abundance in the following food:

- Avocados
- Nuts
- Canola, olive and peanut oils
- Nut-based butter

But don't overdo their intake, as all fats are high in calories and they can cause obesity.

Protein rich ingredients:

Lean meat, shellfish, skinless poultry, eggs, unsalted almonds, soy products like tofu, and legumes are examples of foods high in protein. Legumes like dried beans and lentils, chickpeas, four-bean mix, and kidney beans are also rich in protein, but they also contain carbs, so they may affect your blood glucose levels, so limit their intake. When it comes to meat, diabetic patients can enjoy all sorts of meat but in an appropriate amount. Animal fat should be removed from the meat before consumption. Lean red meat contains minimum fats, and it can be consumed in different meals. Poultry, including chicken, hen, duck, turkey or other birds and seafood, are all allowed on the diabetic diet. In fact, white meat is considered healthier for diabetic patients. The method of their preparation also determines whether they are good to consume or not. If fried or cooked with lots of fats and carbs, the same meat can become far more harmful.

Foods to Avoid or Limit If You Have Type 2 Diabetes

For those with diabetes, it is ineffective to plan a diet in general. They all need to be very clear about the foods they eat every day. There isn't much room for trying out the wrong kinds of ingredients. For these people, eating foods high in carbohydrates is quite unhealthy, so it's important to have a thorough list of these products to avoid them. The foods that are not permitted on a diabetic diet are the following:

Sugars:

Sugar is a simple carbohydrate; once it enters the digestive system, it rapidly breaks down into glucose and spikes the blood glucose level. On a diabetic diet, food that raises blood sugar levels is allowed. The following types of sugars and sweeteners are prohibited:

1. White sugar
2. Brown sugar
3. Confectionary sugar
4. Honey
5. Molasses
6. Granulated sugar

You must first gradually reduce your intake until you are ready to stop altogether. Start incorporating alternative sweeteners like swerve, stevia or erythritol, which are completely carb-free.

High fat dairy products:

Patients with diabetes are more vulnerable to numerous other deadly illnesses, such as cardiovascular ones. Obesity and increased insulin resistance are both caused by high-fat consumption. Foods high in fat should be avoided. On a diabetic diet plan, dairy products like full-fat milk and cream shouldn't be consumed. All dairy products are suitable to use aside from that. Look for low-fat versions of cheese, milk and cream.

Saturated animal fats:

Whether a person has diabetes or not, saturated animal fats are bad for everyone. So, refrain from using. When preparing beef, make an effort to trim off all the extra fat. Avoid using cooking oils that contain these saturated fats. Avoid consuming any lipids of an animal origin. The bad cholesterol or low-density lipoprotein deposits in the vessels, impeding blood flow and hormone production or regulation. This is why foods with high cholesterol levels are bad for diabetes. Replace these things with ones with healthier unsaturated fats.

Sugary drinks:

Colas and other such drinks that contain a lot of sugar are not healthy for anyone, let alone diabetic. Within 30 minutes of drinking such drinks, the blood glucose level might significantly increase. Fortunately, there are several diabetic-friendly drinks with sugar-free options available that you can take. Fresh juices, water and zero-calorie drinks are good options.

Sugar syrups and toppings:

Many of the syrups that are sold in stores are composed entirely of sugar. Maple syrup is a prime example. The patient should stay away from these sugary syrups and store-bought toppings if he is on a diabetic diet. Trust yourself and make them at home using a sugar-free recipe if you wish to use such products at all.

Sweet chocolate and candies:

Sugar-free chocolates are the sole option for diabetics. Their health is seriously threatened by other processed chocolate treats, so these should all be avoided. You can make healthy bars and sweets at home using a recipe that doesn't contain sugar or high glycemic food.

Processed food:

Such foods are filled with salt, sugar, and refined carbohydrates. Because of this reason, processed food is not permitted on a diabetic diet.

Everyday Tips to Stay Healthy

If you haven't been taking your health seriously for most of your life, then after crossing 50, you have to change that attitude. Now your body needs extra care and attention to stay healthy. Besides following a rich and balanced diet, you need major lifestyle changes, and the following suggestions can help you make the most out of your diabetic-friendly diet:

Use the "plate" method:

The American Diabetes Association provides this simple and easy-to-follow meal-planning approach. Basically, it emphasizes eating more vegetables. Take the following actions to prepare your plate per meal:
1. Non-starchy veggies, such as spinach, carrots, and tomatoes, should make up half of your plate.
2. Give a protein, like a tuna, lean pork, or chicken, a quarter of your dish.
3. Add a whole grain, such as brown rice, or a starchy vegetable, like green peas, to the last part of the plate.
4. Include "healthy" fats in moderation, such as those found in nuts or avocados.
5. Include a serving of dairy or fruit along with a glass of water, unsweetened tea, or coffee.

Count your carbs:

Carbohydrates have the most effect on your blood glucose level since they break down into glucose. You might need to learn how to calculate the number of carbohydrates you consume so that you can change the insulin dosage to control your blood sugar. It's critical to monitor the carbohydrate content of each meal and snack. You can learn portion control techniques from a dietitian, who can also help you become a knowledgeable label reader. Additionally, you could learn from him or her how to pay close attention to portion size and carbohydrate content. A nutritionist can show you how to count the number of carbohydrates in each meal and snack if you are taking insulin and how to change your insulin dosage accordingly.

Stay physically active:

It's time to get active if you aren't already. You can cross-train without joining a gym. Play some active video games, go for a stroll, or ride a bike. The majority of the week, you should aim for 30 minutes of exercise that causes you to perspire and breathe more laboriously. You can better manage your diabetes by leading an active lifestyle, which lowers your blood sugar. Additionally, it lessens your risk of developing heart disease. It can help in weight loss and stress reduction.

Monitor your physical health:

It is important to get yourself checked twice or thrice a year. Diabetes slowly progresses to damage other organs and their functions, and with regular checkups, you can manage your health as needed. The risk of developing heart disease is more likely if you have diabetes. Keep on checking your cholesterol, blood pressure, and A1c values after every 3 months. Since diabetes can affect your eyesight, so every year, go for a complete eye exam. To check for issues including nerve damage and foot ulcers, see a foot doctor.

Avoid mental stress:

Stress causes your blood sugar levels to rise. Anxiety may affect how well you control your diabetes. You might neglect to take your medications, exercise, or eat properly. Find ways to relax, whether it be through yoga, deep breathing, or relaxing activities. Talk to an expert and share your feelings to release tension.

Quit smoking:

Diabetes increases your risk of developing conditions like nerve damage, heart disease, eye disease, kidney disease, blood vessel disease, stroke, and foot issues. Your likelihood of developing these issues is increased if you smoke while being diabetic. Smoking can also make it more difficult to exercise. Consult your doctor about quitting options.

Say NO to Alcohol:

Avoiding excessive amounts of beer, wine, and alcoholic beverages may make it easier to manage your blood sugar. Don't go overboard if you decide to drink. According to the American Diabetes Association, men and women who drink should each limit their intake to two drinks per day. Alcohol can cause an excessive rise or fall in blood sugar levels. Before consuming alcohol, check your blood sugar and take precautions to prevent lows. Eat when you're drinking if you have diabetes and use insulin or other medications. Consider this when counting carbohydrates since some beverages, such as wine coolers, may have more of them. It is best for your health if you stop having alcohol at all.

21-Day Meal Plan to Kick Start

Time	Breakfast	Lunch	Dinner	Snacks	Daily Total
Day-1	Apple French Toast + 8 oz. skim milk	Beef Cauliflower Soup	Chili Chicken Tenders + Garlic Onion Rings	½ banana	1145 Calories, 83g Carbs, 48g Sugar
Day-2	Spinach & Crab Frittata + 8 oz. skim milk	Simple Caprese Salad	Crock Pot Juicy Beef Roast + Hot Buffalo Bites	½ cup green grapes	788 Calories, 65g Carbs, 44g Sugar
Day-3	Healthy Apple Walnut Pancakes + 8 oz. skim milk	Butternut Squash Fritters	Asian Sesame Beef Bowls + Fluffy Chocolate Torte	Garlic Pita Crisps	1068 Calories, 95g Carbs, 33g Sugar
Day-4	Blueberry French Toast + 8 oz. unsweetened orange juice	Apple Celery Salad	Spicy Coconut Shrimp + Baked Custard with Maple Syrup	½ cup strawberries	1015 Calories, 100g Carbs, 64g Sugar
Day-5	Vanilla Apple Granola + 8 oz. unsweetened orange juice	Chili Chicken Tenders	Beef Cauliflower Soup + Almond Cheese Bites	Coconut Carrot Cupcakes	1081 Calories, 67g Carbs, 44g Sugar
Day-6	Spinach & Crab Frittata + 8 oz. skim milk	Garlic Chicken Thighs	Seafood Onion Chowder + No Bake Lemon Coconut Tart	Zucchini Fries	1033 Calories, 75g Carbs, 63g Sugar
Day-7	Blueberry French Toast + 8 oz. skim milk	Chili Maple Glazed Salmon	Herbed Pork Tenderloin + ½ cup green beans	Mini Cinnamon Bread Puddings	840 Calories, 54g Carbs, 37g Sugar
Day-8	Cafe Avocado Mocha Smoothies	Lemon Chicken & Peppers	Sirloin Strips & Cauliflower Rice + Soft Lemon Bars	Spicy Mixed Nuts	1012 Calories, 53g Carbs, 34g Sugar
Day-9	Cinnamon Banana Egg Rolls + 8 oz. skim milk	Crab & Carrot Bisque	Cheesy Chicken Salad Casserole + Baked Custard with Maple Syrup	Frozen Pineapple Yogurt	1106 Calories, 88g Carbs, 60g Sugar
Day-10	Healthy Apple Walnut Pancakes + ½ cup green grapes	Korean Chili Chicken	Italian Vegetable Soup + Chili Tortilla Chips	German Chocolate Cake Bars	964 Calories, 92g Carbs, 44g Sugar
Day-11	Hawaiian Ham Breakfast Bake + 8 oz. skim milk	Korean Radish Beef Soup	Lime Chicken Guacamole Salad + Cranberry Watermelon Ice	Nutmeg Apple Chips	810 Calories, 66g Carbs, 44g Sugar
Day-12	Vanilla Apple Granola + 8 oz. skim milk	Chicken Spinach Tuscany	Cajun Beef & Cauliflower Rice Skillet + Coconut Flour Tortillas	Banana Oat Nut Cookies	1100 Calories, 44g Carbs, 22g Sugar

Day-13	Blackberry Cinnamon Muffins + 8 oz. orange juice	Mexican Beef and Tomato Stew	Roasted Duck Legs + Garlic Breadsticks	Lemon Cauliflower Puree	1084 Calories, 80g Carbs, 48g Sugar
Day-14	Healthy Bread Loaf + 8 oz. skim milk	Crock Pot Orange Carnitas	Spicy Fish & Tomatoes + Grilled Stone Fruit	Zucchini Fries	1109 Calories, 69g Carbs, 45g Sugar
Day-15	Breakfast Berry Bark + 8 oz. skim milk	Curried Chicken and Apples	Chili Catfish + Coconut Flour Buns	½ cup strawberries	1051 Calories, 63g Carbs, 42g Sugar
Day-16	Cinnamon Banana Egg Rolls + 8 oz. skim milk	Mayonnaise Chicken Salad	Beef Cauliflower Soup + Cranberry Watermelon Ice	Chili Tortilla Chips	856 Calories, 92g Carbs, 60g Sugar
Day-17	Healthy Apple Walnut Pancakes + 8 oz. orange juice	Asian Pork Meatball Soup	Pan Seared Trout with Lemon + Chinese Chicken Wings	Cinnamon Candied Pecans	1054 Calories, 65g Carbs, 32g Sugar
Day-18	Healthy Bread Loaf + ½ cup green grapes	French Beef Onion Casserole	Creamy Pasta with Tomatoes + Peanut Butter Oatmeal Bars	Mini Cinnamon Bread Puddings	1022 Calories, 87g Carbs, 38g Sugar
Day-19	Almond Breakfast Porridge + 8 oz. skim milk	Cheesy Chicken Salad Casserole	Crunchy Lemon Grilled Chicken + Garlic Onion Rings	Lemon Blueberry Cupcakes	1225 Calories, 83g Carbs, 36g Sugar
Day-20	Vanilla Apple Granola + ½ banana	Pan Seared Trout with Lemon	Crust Feta Broccoli Quiche + Spicy Mixed Nuts	Apple Oat Crisp	1151 Calories, 54g Carbs, 25g Sugar
Day-21	Hawaiian Ham Breakfast Bake + 8 oz. skim milk	BBQ Pork Tacos with Cabbages	Pizza Stuffed Mushroom + Soft Lemon Bars	Grilled Stone Fruit	819 Calories, 78g Carbs, 49g Sugar

Conclusion

A healthy diet can do miracles that no medicines can do; it can help prevent the progression of a disease. A condition like the type 2 diabetes cannot be reversed for good; however, it can be managed through a diet suitable to maintain a healthy blood glucose level and keep your body weight in control. Such a diet must contain only complex carbs, less starch and sugar, and only healthy fats and lean proteins. If you consume all the right nutrients in the right balance every day, you can surely live a healthy life. Now with this diabetic-friendly guide and an extensive recipe collection, you can start that today. Give it a read, pick your favorite recipes and cook something healthy and delicious now!

Quick Apple Cinnamon Scones, page 11

Breakfast Berry Bark, page 11

Apple French Toast, page 11

Blackberry Cinnamon Muffins, page 12

Chapter 2 Breakfast Recipe

Quick Apple Cinnamon Scones

Prep time: 5 minutes, Cook time: 25 minutes, Serves: 16

Ingredients:

2 large eggs
1 apple, diced
¼ cup + ½ tbsp. nut butter, melted and divided
1 tbsp. nonfat half-n-half
What you'll need from store cupboard:
3 cups almond flour
⅓ cup + 2 tsps. swerve
2 tsps. baking powder
2 tsps. cinnamon
1 tsp. vanilla
¼ tsp. salt

Instructions:

1. Heat oven to 325 °F. Line a large baking sheet with parchment paper.
2. In a large bowl, whisk flour, ⅓ cup sweetener, baking powder, 1½ tsps. cinnamon, and salt together. Stir in apple.
3. Add the eggs, ¼ cup melted nut butter, cream, and vanilla. Stir until the mixture forms a soft dough.
4. Divide the dough in half and pat into 2 circles, about 1-inch thick, and 7-8 inches around.
5. In a small bowl, stir together remaining 2 tsps. swerve, and ½ tsp. cinnamon.
6. Brush the ½ tbsp. melted nut butter over dough and sprinkle with cinnamon mixture. Cut each into 8 equal pieces and place on prepared baking sheet.
7. Bake 20-25 minutes, or until golden brown and firm to the touch.

Nutrition Facts Per Serving

Calories 176 Total Carbs 12g Net Carbs 9g Protein 5g Fat 12g Sugar 8g Fiber 3g

Apple French Toast

Prep time: 10 minutes, Cook time: 10 minutes, Serves: 2

Ingredients:

1 apple, peel and slice thin
1 egg
¼ cup skim milk
2 tbsps. nut butter, divided
What you'll need from store cupboard:
4 slices Healthy Loaf Bread
1 tsp. stevia
1 tsp. vanilla
¼ tsp. cinnamon

Instructions:

1. Melt 1 tbsp. nut butter in a large skillet over med-high heat. Add apples, stevia, and cinnamon and cook, stirring frequently, until apples are tender.
2. In a shallow dish, whisk together egg, milk, and vanilla.
3. Melt the remaining nut butter in a separate skillet over med-high heat. Dip each slice of bread in the egg mixture and cook until golden brown on both sides.
4. Place two slices of French toast on plates, and top with apples. Serve immediately.

Nutrition Facts Per Serving

Calories 394 Total Carbs 27g Net Carbs 22g Protein 10g Fat 23g Sugar 19g Fiber 5g

Breakfast Berry Bark

Prep time: 10 minutes, freeze time: 2 hours, Serves: 6

Ingredients:

3-4 strawberries, sliced
1½ cups plain Greek yogurt
½ cup blueberries
What you'll need from store cupboard:
½ cup low fat granola
3 tbsps. sugar free maple syrup

Instructions:

1. Line a baking sheet with parchment paper.
2. In a medium bowl, mix yogurt and syrup until combined. Pour into prepared pan and spread in a thin even layer.
3. Top with remaining ingredients. Cover with foil and freeze two hours or overnight.
4. To serve: slice into squares and serve immediately. If bark thaws too much it will lose its shape. Store any remaining bark in an airtight container in the freezer.

Nutrition Facts Per Serving

Calories 69 Total Carbs 18g Net Carbs 16g Protein 7g Fat 6g Sugar 7g Fiber 2g

Blackberry Cinnamon Muffins

Prep time: 10 minutes, Cook time: 30 minutes, Serves: 10

Ingredients:

3 eggs
1 cup blackberries
⅓ cup nonfat half-n-half
¼ cup nut butter, melted
What you'll need from store cupboard:
1½ cups almond flour
⅓ cup Splenda
1 tsp. baking powder
1 tsp. cinnamon

Instructions:

1. Heat oven to 350 °F. Line 10 muffin cups with paper liners.
2. In a large mixing bowl, combine dry ingredients.
3. Stir in wet ingredients and mix well.
4. Fold in the blackberries and spoon evenly into lined muffin pan.
5. Bake 25-30 minutes or they pass the toothpick test.

Nutrition Facts Per Serving

Calories 194 Total Carbs 12g Net Carbs 10g Protein 5g Fat 14g Sugar 9g Fiber 2g

Healthy Apple Walnut Pancakes

Prep time: 15 minutes, Cook time: 30 minutes, Serves: 18

Ingredients:

1 apple, peeled and diced
2 cups skim milk
2 egg whites
1 egg, beaten
What you'll need from store cupboard:
1 cup flour
1 cup whole wheat flour
½ cup walnuts, chopped
2 tbsps. sunflower oil
1 tbsp. swerve
2 tsps. baking powder
1 tsp. salt
Nonstick cooking spray

Instructions:

1. In a large bowl, combine dry ingredients.
2. In a separate bowl, combine egg whites, egg, milk, and oil and add to dry ingredients. Stir just until moistened. Fold in apple and walnuts.
3. Spray a large griddle with cooking spray and heat. Pour batter, ¼ cup on to hot griddle. Flip when bubbles form on top. Cook until second side is golden brown. Serve with sugar free syrup.

Nutrition Facts Per Serving

Calories 120 Total Carbs 15g Net Carbs 13g Protein 4g Fat 5g Sugar 3g Fiber 2g

Blueberry French Toast

Prep time: 15 minutes, Cook time: 20 minutes, Serves: 8

Ingredients:

4 eggs
1½ cups blueberries
½ cup orange juice
1 tsp. orange zest
What you'll need from store cupboard:
16 slices bread
3 tbsps. Splenda, divided
⅛ tsp. salt
Orange Blueberry Dessert Sauce, (chapter 13)
Nonstick cooking spray

Instructions:

1. Heat oven to 400 °F. Spray a large baking sheet with cooking spray.
2. In a small bowl, combine berries with 2 tbsps. of Splenda.
3. Lay 8 slices of bread on work surface. Top with about 3 tbsps. of berries and place second slice of bread on top. Flatten slightly.
4. In a shallow dish, whisk remaining ingredients together. Carefully dip both sides of bread in egg mixture and place on prepared pan.
5. Bake 7-12 minutes per side, or until lightly browned.
6. Heat up dessert sauce until warm. Plate the French toast and top with 1-2 tbsps. of the sauce. Serve.

Nutrition Facts Per Serving

Calories 208 Total Carbs 20g Net Carbs 18g Protein 7g Fat 10g Sugar 14g Fiber 2g

Cafe Avocado Mocha Smoothies

Total time: 5 minutes, Serves: 3

Ingredients:

1 avocado, remove pit and cut in half
1½ cups almond milk, unsweetened
½ cup canned coconut milk
What you'll need from store cupboard:
3 tbsps. Splenda
3 tbsps. unsweetened cocoa powder
2 tsps. instant coffee
1 tsp. vanilla

Instructions:

1. Place everything but the avocado in the blender. Process until smooth.
2. Add the avocado and blend until smooth and no chunks remain.
3. Pour into glasses and serve.

Nutrition Facts Per Serving

Calories 109 Total Carbs 15g Net Carbs 12g Protein 6g Fat 1g Sugar 13g Fiber 0g

Vanilla Apple Granola

Prep time: 5 minutes, Cook time: 35 minutes, Serves: 4

Ingredients:

1 apple, peel and dice fine
¼ cup nut butter, melted
What you'll need from store cupboard:
1 cup walnuts or pecans
1 cup almond flour
¾ cup flaked coconut
½ cup sunflower seeds
½ cup hemp seeds
⅓ cup Splenda
2 tsps. cinnamon
2 tsps. vanilla
½ tsp. salt

Instructions:

1. Heat oven to 300 °F. Line a large baking sheet with parchment paper.
2. Place the nuts, flour, coconut, seeds, Splenda, and salt in a food processor. Pulse until mixture resembles coarse crumbs but leave some chunks.
3. Transfer to a bowl and add apple and cinnamon. Stir in nut butter and vanilla until well coated and mixture starts to clump together.
4. Pour onto prepared pan and spread out evenly. Bake 25 minutes, stirring a couple of times, until it starts to brown.
5. Turn the oven off and let granola sit inside 5-10 minutes. Remove from oven and cool completely, it will crisp up more as it cools. Store in airtight container.

Nutrition Facts Per Serving

Calories 360 Total Carbs 19g Net Carbs 14g Protein 10g Fat 28g Sugar 12g Fiber 5g

Cinnamon Banana Egg Rolls

Prep time: 15 minutes, Cook time: 20 minutes, Serves: 6

Ingredients:

4 eggs
1 ripe banana
What you'll need from store cupboard:
⅔ cup coconut flour
3 drops liquid stevia, divided
6 tbsps. coconut oil, soft, divided
1 tsp. vanilla
1 tsp. baking soda
½ tsp. salt
1 tbsp. + ½ tsp. cinnamon

Instructions:

1. Heat oven to 350 °F. Line a cookie sheet with parchment paper.
2. In a medium bowl, lightly beat eggs. Beat in the banana. Add 1 drop liquid stevia, 2 tbsps. melted coconut oil, and vanilla and mix to combine.
3. Mix in flour, salt, baking soda, and ½ tsp. cinnamon until thoroughly combined. If dough is too sticky add more flour, a little at a time.
4. Line a work surface with parchment paper and place dough on top. Place another sheet of parchment paper on top and roll out into a large rectangle.
5. In a small bowl, combine 1 drop liquid stevia, 2 tbsps. coconut oil, and 1 tbsps. of cinnamon and spread on dough.
6. Roll up and cut into 6 equal pieces. Place on prepared pan and bake 15-30 minutes, or until golden brown.
7. Let cool 10 minutes. Stir together the remaining 1 drop liquid stevia and 2 tbsps coconut oil and spread over warm rolls. Serve.

Nutrition Facts Per Serving

Calories 247 Total Carbs 23g Net Carbs 18g Protein 4g Fat 17g Sugar 20g Fiber 1g

Almond Breakfast Porridge

Prep time: 2 minutes, Cook time: 10 minutes, Serves: 4

Ingredients:

4 cups vanilla almond milk, unsweetened
What you'll need from store cupboard:
1 cup unsweetened coconut, grated
8 tsps. coconut flour
¼ cup blueberries

Instructions:

1. Add coconut to a saucepan and cook over med-high heat until it is lightly toasted. Be careful not to let it burn.
2. Add milk and bring to a boil. While stirring, slowly add flour, cook and stir until mixture starts to thicken, about 5 minutes.
3. Remove from heat, mixture will thicken more as it cools. Ladle into bowls, add blueberries, or drizzle with a little liquid stevia if desired.

Nutrition Facts Per Serving

Calories 231 Total Carbs 21g Net Carbs 8g Protein 6g Fat 14g Sugar 4g Fiber 13g

Spinach & Crab Frittata

Prep time: 10 minutes, Cook time: 30 minutes, Serves: 10

Ingredients:

¾ lb. crabmeat
8 eggs
10 oz. spinach, frozen and thawed, squeeze dry
2 stalks celery, diced
2 cups nonfat half-n-half
1 cup Swiss cheese
½ cup onion, diced
½ cup red pepper, diced
¼ cup mushrooms, diced
2 tbsps. nut butter
What you'll need from store cupboard:
1 cup bread crumbs
½ tsp. salt
¼ tsp. pepper
¼ tsp. nutmeg
Nonstick cooking spray

Instructions:

1. Heat oven to 375 °F. Spray a large casserole, or baking dish with cooking spray.
2. In a large bowl, beat eggs and half-n-half. Stir in crab, spinach, bread crumbs, cheese, and seasonings.
3. Melt butter in a large skillet over medium heat. Add celery, onion, rep pepper, and mushrooms. Cook, stirring occasionally, until vegetables are tender, about 5 minutes. Add to egg mixture.
4. Pour mixture into prepared baking dish and bake 30-35 minutes, or until eggs are set and top is light brown. Cool 10 minutes before serving.

Nutrition Facts Per Serving

Calories 261 Total Carbs 18g Net Carbs 16g Protein 14g Fat 15g Sugar 4g Fiber 2g

Strawberry Mango Smoothies

Prep time: 5 minutes, Total time: 10 minutes, Serves: 2

Ingredients:

½ mango, peeled and diced
¾ cup strawberries, halved
½ cup skim milk
¼ cup vanilla yogurt
What you'll need from store cupboard:
3 ice cubes
2 tsps. Splenda

Instructions:

1. Combine all ingredients in a blender. Process until smooth. Pour into chilled glasses and serve immediately.

Nutrition Facts Per Serving

Calories 132 Total Carbs 26g Net Carbs 24g Protein 5g Fat 1g Sugar 23g Fiber 2g

Hawaiian Ham Breakfast Bake

Prep time: 10 minutes, Cook time: 20 minutes, Serves: 6

Ingredients:

6 slices ham, sliced thin
6 eggs
¼ cup reduced fat cheddar cheese, grated
What you'll need from store cupboard:
6 pineapple slices
2 tbsps. salsa
½ tsp. seasoning blend, salt-free

Instructions:

1. Heat oven to 350 °F.
2. Line 6 muffin cups, or ramekins with sliced ham. Layer with cheese, salsa, and pineapple.
3. Crack one egg into each cup, sprinkle with seasoning blend.
4. If using ramekins place them on a baking sheet, bake 20-25 minutes or until egg whites are completely set but yolks are still soft. Serve immediately.

Nutrition Facts Per Serving

Calories 135 Total Carbs 5g Net Carbs 4g Protein 12g Fat 8g Sugar 3g Fiber 1g

Ham and Cheese Breakfast Biscuits

Prep time: 5 minutes, Cook time: 15 minutes, Serves: 4

Ingredients:

1 cup ham, diced
2 eggs
¾ cup mozzarella cheese, grated
½ cup low fat cheddar cheese, grated
What you'll need from store cupboard:
½ cup reduced fat grated parmesan, grated

Instructions:

1. Heat oven to 375 °F. Line a baking sheet with parchment paper.
2. In a large bowl, combine the cheeses and eggs until fully combined. Stir in the ham.
3. Divide the mixture evenly into 8 parts and form into round tolls. Bake 15-20 minutes or until cheese is completely melted and the rolls are nicely browned.

Nutrition Facts Per Serving

Calories 192 Total Carbs 2g Net Carbs 1g Protein 16g Fat 13g Sugar 0g Fiber 0g

Butternut Squash Fritters, page 16

Crust Feta Broccoli Quiche, page 16

Cauliflower and Mushroom Risotto, page 16

Pizza Stuffed Mushroom, page 17

Butternut Squash Fritters

Ingredients:

5 cups butternut squash, grated
2 large eggs
1 tbsp. fresh sage, diced fine
What you'll need from store cupboard:
⅔ cup flour
2 tbsps. olive oil
Salt and pepper, to taste

Instructions:

1. Heat oil in a large skillet over med-high heat.
2. In a large bowl, combine squash, eggs, sage and salt and pepper to taste. Fold in flour.
3. Drop ¼ cup mixture into skillet, keeping fritters at least 1 inch apart. Cook till golden brown on both sides, about 2 minutes per side.
4. Transfer to paper towel lined plate. Repeat. Serve immediately with your favorite dipping sauce.

Nutrition Facts Per Serving

Calories 164 Total Carbs 24g Net Carbs 21g Protein 4g Fat 6g Sugar 3g Fiber 3g

Cauliflower and Mushroom Risotto

Ingredients:

1 medium head cauliflower, grated
8 oz. Porcini mushrooms, sliced
1 yellow onion, diced fine
What you'll need from store cupboard:
2 cups low sodium vegetable broth
2 tsps. garlic, diced fine
2 tsps. white wine vinegar
Salt & pepper, to taste
Olive oil cooking spray

Instructions:

1. Heat oven to 350 °F. Line a baking sheet with foil.
2. Place the mushrooms on the prepared pan and spray with cooking spray. Sprinkle with salt and toss to coat. Bake 10-12 minutes, or until golden brown and the mushrooms start to crisp.
3. Spray a large skillet with cooking spray and place over med-high heat. Add onion and cook, stirring frequently, until translucent, about 3-4 minutes. Add garlic and cook 2 minutes, until golden.
4. Add the cauliflower and cook 1 minute, stirring.

5. Place the broth in a saucepan and bring to a simmer. Add to the skillet, ¼ cup at a time, mixing well after each addition.
6. Stir in vinegar. Reduce heat to low and let simmer, 4-5 minutes, or until most of the liquid has evaporated.
7. Spoon cauliflower mixture onto plates, or in bowls, and top with mushrooms. Serve.

Nutrition Facts Per Serving

Calories 134 Total Carbs 22g Net Carbs 19g Protein 10g Fat 0g Sugar 5g Fiber 2g

Crust Feta Broccoli Quiche

Ingredients:

3 large eggs
2 cups broccoli florets, chopped
1 small onion, diced
1 cup cheddar cheese, grated
⅔ cup unsweetened almond milk
½ cup feta cheese, crumbled
What you'll need from store cupboard:
1 tbsp. extra virgin olive oil
½ tsp. sea salt
¼ tsp. black pepper
Nonstick cooking spray

Instructions:

1. Heat oven to 350 °F. Spray a 9-inch baking dish with cooking spray.
2. Heat the oil in a large skillet over medium heat. Add onion and cook 4-5 minutes, until onions are translucent.
3. Add broccoli and stir to combine. Cook until broccoli turns a bright green, about 2 minutes. Transfer to a bowl.
4. In a small bowl, whisk together almond milk, egg, salt, and pepper. Pour over the broccoli. Add the cheddar cheese and stir the ingredients together. Pour into the prepared baking dish.
5. Sprinkle the feta cheese over the top and bake 45 minutes to 1 hour, or until eggs are set in the middle and top is lightly browned. Serve.

Nutrition Facts Per Serving

Calories 182 Total Carbs 5g Net Carbs 4g Protein 10g Fat 14g Sugar 2g Fiber 1g

Pizza Stuffed Mushroom

Prep time: 5 minutes, Cook time: 10 minutes, Serves: 4

Ingredients:

8 Portobello mushrooms, stems removed
1 cup mozzarella cheese, grated
1 cup cherry tomatoes, sliced
½ cup crushed tomatoes
½ cup fresh basil, chopped
What you'll need from store cupboard:
2 tbsps. balsamic vinegar
1 tbsp. olive oil
1 tbsp. oregano
1 tbsp. red pepper flakes
½ tbsp. garlic powder
¼ tsp. pepper
Pinch salt

Instructions:

1. Heat oven to broil. Line a baking sheet with foil.
2. Place mushrooms, stem side down, on foil and drizzle with oil. Sprinkle with garlic powder, salt and pepper. Broil for 5 minutes.
3. Flip mushrooms over and top with crushed tomatoes, oregano, parsley, pepper flakes, cheese and sliced tomatoes. Broil another 5 minutes.
4. Top with basil and drizzle with balsamic. Serve.

Nutrition Facts Per Serving

Calories 113 Total Carbs 11g Net Carbs 7g Protein 9g Fat 5g Sugar 3g Fiber 4g

Creamy Pasta with Tomatoes

Prep time: 10 minutes, Cook time: 10 minutes, Serves: 4

Ingredients:

4 tomatoes, deseeded & diced
4 oz. fat free cream cheese, cut in cubes
1 cup peas, thawed
½ cup skim milk
4 tbsps. fresh parsley, diced
What you'll need from store cupboard:
½ recipe Homemade Pasta, cook & drain, (chapter 4)
4 cloves garlic, diced fine
3 tbsps. olive oil
1 tsp. oregano
1 tsp. basil
½ tsp. garlic salt

Instructions:

1. Heat oil in a large skillet over medium heat. Add garlic and tomatoes, cook 3-4 minutes, stirring frequently.
2. Add peas, milk, cream cheese, and seasonings. Cook, stirring, 5 minutes, or until cream cheese has melted.
3. Add pasta and toss to coat. Serve garnished with parsley.

Nutrition Facts Per Serving

Calories 332 Total Carbs 19g Net Carbs 14g Protein 14g Fat 23g Sugar 10g Fiber 5g

Eggplant and Zucchini Parmesan

Prep time: 10 minutes, Cook time: 2 hours, Serves: 6

Ingredients:

1 medium eggplant, peeled and cut into 1-inch cubes
1 medium zucchini, cut into 1-inch pieces
1 medium onion, cut into thin wedges
What you'll need from store cupboard:
1½ cups purchased light spaghetti sauce
⅔ cup reduced fat parmesan cheese, grated

Instructions:

1. Place the vegetables, spaghetti sauce and ⅓ cup parmesan in the crock pot. Stir to combine. Cover and cook on high 2-2½ hours, or on low 4-5 hours.
2. Sprinkle remaining parmesan on top before serving.

Nutrition Facts Per Serving

Calories 81 Total Carbs 12g Net Carbs 7g Protein 5g Fat 2g Sugar 7g Fiber 5g

Florentine Spinach Pizza

Prep time: 15 minutes, Cook time: 20 minutes, Serves: 2

Ingredients:

1¾ cups grated mozzarella cheese
½ cup frozen spinach, thaw
1 egg
2 tbsps. reduced fat parmesan cheese, grated
2 tbsps. cream cheese, soft
What you'll need from store cupboard:
¾ cup almond flour
¼ cup light Alfredo sauce
½ tsp. Italian seasoning
¼ tsp. red pepper flakes
Pinch of salt

Instructions:

1. Heat oven to 400 °F.
2. Squeeze all the excess water out of the spinach.
3. In a glass bowl, combine mozzarella and almond flour. Stir in cream cheese. Microwave 1 minute on high, then stir. If the mixture is not melted, microwave another 30 seconds.
4. Stir in the egg, seasoning, and salt. Mix well. Place dough on a piece of parchment paper and press into a 10-inch circle.
5. Place directly on the oven rack and bake 8-10 minutes or until lightly browned.
6. Remove the crust and spread with the Alfredo sauce, then add spinach, parmesan and red pepper flakes evenly over top. Bake another 8-10 minutes. Slice and serve.

Nutrition Facts Per Serving

Calories 441 Total Carbs 14g Net Carbs 9g Protein 24g Fat 35g Sugar 4g Fiber 5g

Grilled Portobello & Zucchini Sandwich

Prep time: 5 minutes, Cook time: 10 minutes, Serves: 2

Ingredients:

2 large portabella mushroom caps
½ small zucchini, sliced
2 slices low fat cheese
¼ cup spinach
What you'll need from store cupboard:
2 100% whole wheat sandwich thins
2 tsps. roasted red bell peppers
2 tsps. olive oil

Instructions:

1. Heat grill, or charcoal, to med-high heat.
2. Lightly brush mushroom caps with olive oil. Grill mushroom caps and zucchini slices until tender, about 3-4 minutes per side.
3. Place on sandwich thin. Top with sliced cheese, roasted red bell pepper, and spinach. Serve.

Nutrition Facts Per Serving

Calories 177 Total Carbs 26g Net Carbs 22g Protein 15g Fat 3g Sugar 3g Fiber 8g

Cauliflower and Pepper Casserole

Prep time: 15 minutes, Cook time: 30 minutes, Serves: 12

Ingredients:

1 head cauliflower, grated
1 red bell pepper, diced fine
1 green bell pepper, diced fine
1 jalapeno pepper, seeded and diced fine
½ white onion, diced fine
1½ cups cheddar cheese, grated
1 tsp. cilantro, diced fine
What you'll need from store cupboard:
½ cup salsa
3 tbsps. water
1 tsp. chili powder
Nonstick cooking spray

Instructions:

1. Heat oven to 350 °F. Spray a 7x11x2-inch baking pan with cooking spray.
2. In a large skillet, over medium heat, cook onions and peppers until soft, about 5 minutes. Add cilantro and chili powder and stir.
3. Place the cauliflower and water in a glass bowl and microwave on high for 3 minutes. Stir in 1 cup cheese and the salsa.
4. Stir the pepper mixture into the cauliflower and combine. Spread in prepared pan. Sprinkle the remaining cheese over the top and bake 30-35 minutes.
5. Let rest 5 minutes before cutting into 12 squares and serving.

Nutrition Facts Per Serving

Calories 74 Total Carbs 4g Net Carbs 3g Protein 4g Fat 5g Sugar 2g Fiber 1g

Dill Zucchini Fritters

Prep time: 40 minutes, Cook time: 10 minutes, Serves: 4

Ingredients:

3 zucchinis, grated
2 eggs
1 onion, diced
¾ cups feta cheese, crumbled
¼ cup fresh dill, chopped
1 tbsp. nut butter
What you'll need from store cupboard:
½ cup flour
1 tsp. salt
Pepper to taste
Oil for frying

Instructions:

1. Place zucchini in a large colander and sprinkle with the salt. Toss with fingers and let sit 30 minutes. Squeeze with back of spoon to remove the excess water. Place the zucchini between paper towels and squeeze again. Place in large bowl and let dry.
2. Melt nut butter in a large skillet over med-high heat. Add onion and cook until soft, about 5 minutes. Add to zucchini along with the feta and dill and mix well.
3. In a small bowl, whisk together the flour and eggs. Pour over zucchini and mix well.
4. Add oil to the skillet to equal ½-inch and heat over med-high heat until very hot. Drop golf ball sized scoops of zucchini mixture into oil and flatten into a patty. Cook until golden brown on both sides. Transfer to paper towel line plate.
5. Serve with sauce of your choice.

Nutrition Facts Per Serving

Calories 253 Total Carbs 21g Net Carbs 18g Protein 10g Fat 15g Sugar 5g Fiber 3g

Flourless Burger Buns, page 19

Cauliflower Rice, page 19

Homemade Pasta, page 19

Coconut Flour Tortillas, page 20

Flourless Burger Buns

Prep time: 10 minutes, Cook time: 35 minutes, Serves: 4

Ingredients:

4 egg yolks, room temp
4 egg whites, room temp
¼ cup low fat ricotta cheese
What you'll need from store cupboard:
¼ cup reduced fat parmesan cheese
¼ tsp. cream of tartar

Instructions:

1. Heat oven to 300 °F. Line a baking sheet with parchment paper.
2. In a large bowl, whisk egg yolks, ricotta and parmesan cheese until smooth.
3. In a separate bowl, beat egg whites until foamy, then add in cream of tartar and beat until stiff peaks form.
4. Add some beaten egg white to the egg yolk mixture and mix lightly. Slowly and lightly fold in the remaining egg white to the egg yolk mixture until just blended.
5. Spoon the batter onto prepared pan to make 8 buns. Bake 35 minutes. Use as bread for sandwiches or eat on its own.

Nutrition Facts Per Serving

Calories 50 Total Carbs 1g Net Carbs 0g Protein 4g Fat 3g Sugar 1g Fiber 0g

Homemade Pasta

Prep time: 20 minutes, Cook time: 5 minutes, Serves: 8

Ingredients:

1 egg + 2 egg yolks
What you'll need from store cupboard:
1¾ cups soy flour
¼ cup ground wheat germ
3-4 tbsps. cold water
1 tsp. light olive oil
½ tsp. salt

Instructions:

1. In a large bowl, whisk egg, egg yolks, oil and 3 tbsps. water until smooth.
2. In a separate bowl, combine flour, wheat germ, and salt. Stir into egg mixture until smooth. Use the last tbsp. of water if needed to make a smooth dough.
3. Turn out onto a lightly floured surface and knead 5-8 minutes or until smooth. Cover and let rest 10 minutes.

4. Divide dough into 4 equal pieces and roll out, one at a time, as thin as possible, or run it through a pasta machine until it reaches the thinnest setting.
5. Let dough dry out for 30 minutes. Cut into desired size with pasta machine or pizza cutter. It not using right away, let it dry overnight on a pasta or cooling rack. Fresh pasta should be used within 3 days.
6. It will store in the freezer, after drying for just an hour, in an airtight bag, 6-8 months. Pasta dried overnight can be stored in an airtight container for up to 1 week.
7. To cook it when fresh, add to a pot of boiling water for 4-5 minutes or until tender. Dried pasta will take a couple minutes longer.

Nutrition Facts Per Serving

Calories 152 Total Carbs 12g Net Carbs 9g Protein 16g Fat 5g Sugar 6g Fiber 3g

Cauliflower Rice

Prep time: 5 minutes, Cook time: 10 minutes, Serves: 4

Ingredients:

1 small head cauliflower, separated into small florets
What you'll need from store cupboard:
1 tbsp. olive oil
1 clove of garlic, diced fine
½ tsp. salt

Instructions:

1. Use a cheese grater to rice the cauliflower, using the big holes. Or, use a food processor and short pulses until it resembles rice.
2. In a nonstick skillet, over med-high heat, heat oil until hot. Add garlic and cook 1 minutes, stirring frequently. Add cauliflower and cook, stirring, 7-9 minutes, or until it is tender and starts to brown.
3. Serve as is or use in your favorite recipes.

Nutrition Facts Per Serving

Calories 48, Total Carbs 4g Net Carbs 2g Protein 1g Fat 4g Sugar 2g Fiber 2g

Coconut Flour Tortillas

Prep time: 10 minutes, cook time 15 minutes, Serves: 4

Ingredients:

¾ cup egg whites
What you'll need from store cupboard:
⅓ cup water
¼ cup coconut flour
1 tsp. sunflower oil
½ tsp. salt
½ tsp. cumin
½ tsp. chili powder

Instructions:

1. Add all ingredients, except oil, to a food processor and pulse until combined. Let rest 7-8 minutes.
2. Heat oil in a large skillet over med-low heat. Pour ¼ cup batter into center and tilt to spread to 7-8-inch circle.
3. When the top is no longer shiny, flip tortilla and cook another 1-2 minutes. Repeat with remaining batter.
4. Place each tortilla on parchment paper and slightly wipe off any access oil.

Calories 27 Total Carbs 1g Net Carbs 0g Protein 5g Fat 0g Sugar 0g Fiber 0g

Homemade Noodles

Prep time: 5 minutes, Chill time: 4 hours, Serves: 2

Ingredients:

1 cup mozzarella cheese, grated
1 egg yolk

Instructions:

1. Add the mozzarella to a bowl and microwave for 1-2 minutes, until melted. Let cool for 30 seconds.
2. With a rubber spatula, gently fold the egg yolk into the cheese.
3. Turn the mixture out onto a parchment paper-lined baking sheet. Place another piece of parchment paper on top of the dough and press down with your hand until thin.
4. Remove the top piece of parchment and cut the dough into thin strips. Place the "pasta" on a rack and refrigerate for four hours or overnight.
5. To cook, place in boiling water for 1 minute. Drain and run cool water over to prevent sticking. Serve with your favorite sauce.

Calories 67 Total Carbs 1g Net Carbs 0g Protein 5g Fat 5g Sugar 0g Fiber 0g

Fried Rice with Snap Peas

Prep time: 5 minutes, Cook time: 15 minutes, Serves: 8

Ingredients:

2 cups sugar snap peas
2 egg whites
1 egg
What you'll need from store cupboard:
1 cup instant brown rice, cooked according to directions
2 tbsps. lite soy sauce

Instructions:

1. Add the peas to the cooked rice and mix to combine.
2. In a small skillet, scramble the egg and egg whites. Add the rice and peas to the skillet and stir in soy sauce. Cook, stirring frequently, about 2-3 minutes, or until heated through. Serve.

Calories 107 Total Carbs 20g Net Carbs 19g Protein 4g Fat 1g Sugar 1g Fiber 1g

Garlic Breadsticks

Prep time: 10 minutes, Cook time: 10 minutes, Serves: 4

Ingredients:

2 eggs, beaten
2 cups mozzarella cheese, grated
2 tbsps. low-fat cream cheese
2 tbsps. fresh basil, diced
What you'll need from store cupboard:
4 tbsps. coconut flour
4 cloves garlic, crushed
Nonstick cooking spray

Instructions:

1. Heat oven to 400 °F. Spray a baking sheet with cooking spray.
2. Add mozzarella, cream cheese, crushed garlic and basil to a microwaveable bowl. Mix and then cook for 1 minute. Stir well to make sure the cheeses are melted and then add in the flour and egg.
3. Mix well, use your hands if needed to form into a dough.
4. Break off pieces of the dough and roll into a long finger shapes. Place on prepared pan.
5. Bake 8-10 minutes or until the dough begins to brown. Remove from heat and let cool slightly before serving.

Calories 153 Total Carbs 10g Net Carbs 5g Protein 9g Fat 8g Sugar 1g Fiber 5g

Healthy Bread Loaf

Prep time: 10 minutes, Cook time: 30 minutes, Serves: 20

Ingredients:

6 eggs, separated
4 tbsps. nut butter, melted
What you'll need from store cupboard:
1½ cups almond flour, sifted
3 tsps. baking powder
¼ tsp. cream of tartar
⅛ tsp. salt
Butter flavored cooking spray

Instructions:

1. Heat oven to 375 °F. Spray an 8-inch loaf pan with cooking spray.
2. In a large bowl, beat egg whites and cream of tartar until soft peaks form
3. Add the yolks, ⅓ of egg whites, butter, flour, baking powder, and salt to a food processor and pulse until combined.
4. Add remaining egg whites and pulse until thoroughly combined, being careful not to over mix the dough.
5. Pour into prepared pan and bake 30 minutes, or until bread passes the toothpick test. Cool 10 minutes in the pan then invert and cool completely before slicing.

Nutrition Facts Per Serving

Calories 81 Total Carbs 2g Net Carbs 1g Protein 3g Fat 7g Sugar 0g Fiber 1g

Coconut Flour Buns

Prep time: 5 minutes, Cook time: 20 minutes, Serves: 4

Ingredients:

3 eggs, room temperature
2 tbsps. coconut milk, room temperature
What you'll need from store cupboard:
¼ cup coconut flour
2 tbsps. coconut oil, soft
¼ tsp. stevia
½ tsp. baking powder
½ tsp. salt

Instructions:

1. Heat oven to 375 °F. Line a cookie sheet with parchment paper.
2. In a small bowl, sift together flour, baking powder and salt.
3. In a medium bowl, combine eggs, coconut oil, milk, and stevia, mix well. Slowly add dry ingredients to the egg mixture. Batter will be thick but make sure there is no lumps.
4. Form into 4 balls and place on prepared pan. Press down into rounds ½-inch thick. Bake 15-20 minutes or until buns pass the toothpick test.

Nutrition Facts Per Serving

Calories 143 Total Carbs 6g Net Carbs 5g Protein 4g Fat 12g Sugar 5g Fiber 0g

Simple Caprese Salad , page 24

Lime Chicken Guacamole Salad , page 24

Apple Celery Salad , page 24

Chopped Cucumber and Tomato Salad , page 24

Chapter 5 Salads Recipe

Simple Caprese Salad

Total time: 10 minutes, Serves: 4

Ingredients:
3 medium tomatoes, cut into 8 slices
2 (1-oz.) slices mozzarella cheese, cut into strips
¼ cup fresh basil, sliced thin
What you'll need from store cupboard:
2 tsps. extra-virgin olive oil
⅛ tsp. salt
Pinch black pepper

Instructions:
1. Place tomatoes and cheese on serving plates. Sprinkle with salt and pepper. Drizzle oil over and top with basil. Serve.

Nutrition Facts Per Serving

Calories 77 Total Carbs 4g Net Carbs 2g Protein 5g Fat 5g Sugar 2g Fiber 1g

Apple Celery Salad

Prep time: 5 minutes, Total time: 15 minutes, Serves: 4

Ingredients:
2 green onions, diced
2 Medjool dates, pitted & diced fine
1 honey crisp apple, sliced thin
2 cups celery, sliced
½ cup celery leaves, diced
What you'll need from store cupboard:
¼ cup walnuts, chopped
Maple Shallot Vinaigrette, (chapter 13)

Instructions:
1. Heat oven to 375 °F. Place walnuts on a cookie sheet and bake 10 minutes, stirring every few minutes, to toast.
2. In a large bowl, combine all ingredients and toss to mix.
3. Drizzle vinaigrette over and toss to coat. Serve immediately.

Nutrition Facts Per Serving

Calories 171 Total Carbs 25g Net Carbs 21g Protein 3g Fat 8g Sugar 15g Fiber 4g

Lime Chicken Guacamole Salad

Prep time: 10 minutes, Cook time: 20 minutes, Serves: 6

Ingredients:
1 lb. chicken breast, boneless & skinless
2 avocados
1-2 jalapeno peppers, seeded & diced
⅓ cup onion, diced
3 tbsps. cilantro, diced
2 tbsps. fresh lime juice
What you'll need from store cupboard:
2 cloves garlic, diced
1 tbsp. olive oil
Salt & pepper, to taste

Instructions:
1. Heat oven to 400 °F. Line a baking sheet with foil.
2. Season chicken with salt and pepper and place on prepared pan. Bake 20 minutes, or until chicken is cooked through. Let cool completely.
3. Once chicken has cooled, shred or dice and add to a large bowl. Add remaining ingredients and mix well, mashing the avocado as you mix it in. Taste and season with salt and pepper as desired. Serve immediately.

Nutrition Facts Per Serving

Calories 324 Total Carbs 12g Net Carbs 5g Protein 23g Fat 22g Sugar 1g Fiber 7g

Chopped Cucumber and Tomato Salad

Total time: 15 minutes, Serves: 4

Ingredients:
1 cucumber, chopped
1 pint cherry tomatoes, cut in half
3 radishes, chopped
1 yellow bell pepper chopped
½ cup fresh parsley, chopped
What you'll need from store cupboard:
3 tbsps. lemon juice
1 tbsp. olive oil
Salt to taste

Instructions:
1. Place all ingredients in a large bowl and toss to combine. Serve immediately, or cover and chill until ready to serve.

Nutrition Facts Per Serving

Calories 70 Total Carbs 9g Net Carbs 7g Protein 2g Fat 4g Sugar 5g Fiber 2g

Asian Style Noodle Slaw

Prep time: 5 minutes, Chill time: 2 hours, Serves: 8

Ingredients:

1 lb. bag coleslaw mix
5 scallions, sliced
What you'll need from store cupboard:
1 cup sunflower seeds
1 cup almonds, sliced
3 oz. ramen noodles, broken into small pieces
¾ cup vegetable oil
½ cup Splenda
⅓ cup vinegar

Instructions:

1. In a large bowl, combine coleslaw, sunflower seeds, almonds, and scallions.
2. Whisk together the oil, vinegar and Splenda in a large measuring cup. Pour over salad, and stir to combine.
3. Stir in ramen noodles, cover and chill 2 hours.

Nutrition Facts Per Serving

Calories 354 Total Carbs 24g Net Carbs 21g Protein 5g Fat 26g Sugar 10g Fiber 3g

Autumn Cabbage Slaw

Prep time: 15 minutes, Chill time: 2 hours, Serves: 8

Ingredients:

10 cups cabbage, shredded
½ red onion, diced fine
¾ cup fresh Italian parsley, chopped
What you'll need from store cupboard:
¾ cup almonds, slice & toasted
¾ cup dried cranberries
⅓ cup vegetable oil
¼ cup apple cider vinegar
2 tbsps. sugar free maple syrup
4 tsps. Dijon mustard
½ tsp. salt
Salt & pepper, to taste

Instructions:

1. In a large bowl, whisk together vinegar, oil, syrup, Dijon, and ½ tsp. salt. Add the onion and stir to combine. Let rest 10 minutes, or cover and refrigerate until ready to use.
2. After 10 minutes, add remaining ingredients to the dressing mixture and toss to coat. Taste and season with salt and pepper if needed. Cover and chill 2 hours before serving.

Nutrition Facts Per Serving

Calories 133 Total Carbs 12g Net Carbs 8g Protein 2g Fat 9g Sugar 5g Fiber 4g

Broccoli & Mushroom and Tomato Salad

Total time: 10 minutes, Serves: 4

Ingredients:

4 sun-dried tomatoes, cut in half
3 cups torn leaf lettuce
1½ cups broccoli florets
1 cup mushrooms, sliced
⅓ cup radishes, sliced
What you'll need from store cupboard:
2 tbsps. water
1 tbsp. balsamic vinegar
1 tsp. vegetable oil
¼ tsp. chicken bouillon granules
¼ tsp. parsley
¼ tsp. dry mustard
⅛ tsp. cayenne pepper

Instructions:

1. Place tomatoes in a small bowl and pour boiling water over, just enough to cover. Let stand 5 minutes, drain.
2. Chop tomatoes and place in a large bowl. Add lettuce, broccoli, mushrooms, and radishes.
3. In a jar with a tight fitting lid, add remaining ingredients and shake well. Pour over salad and toss to coat. Serve.

Nutrition Facts Per Serving

Calories 54, Total Carbs 9g Net Carbs 7g Protein 3g Fat 2g Sugar 2g Fiber 2g

Creamy Crab Cabbage Slaw

Prep time: 10 minutes, Chill time: 1 hour, Serves: 4

Ingredients:

½ lb. cabbage, shredded
½ lb. red cabbage, shredded
2 hard-boiled eggs, chopped
Juice of ½ lemon
What you'll need from store cupboard:
2 (6 oz.) cans crabmeat, drained
½ cup lite mayonnaise
1 tsp. celery seeds
Salt & pepper, to taste

Instructions:

1. In a large bowl, combine both kinds of cabbage.
2. In a small bowl, combine mayonnaise, lemon juice, and celery seeds. Add to cabbage and toss to coat.
3. Add crab and eggs and toss to mix, season with salt and pepper. Cover and refrigerate 1 hour before serving.

Nutrition Facts Per Serving

Calories 380 Total Carbs 25g Net Carbs 17g Protein 18g Fat 24g Sugar 13g Fiber 8g

Taco Beef Salad

Prep time: 15 minutes, Cook time: 10 minutes, Serves: 4

Ingredients:

2 whole Romaine hearts, chopped
1 lb. lean ground beef
1 whole avocado, cubed
3 oz. grape tomatoes, halved
½ cup cheddar cheese, cubed
2 tbsps. sliced red onion
What you'll need from store cupboard:
½ batch Tangy Mexican Salad Dressing (chapter 13)
1 tsp. ground cumin
Salt and pepper to taste

Instructions:

1. Cook ground beef in a skillet over medium heat. Break the beef up into little pieces as it cooks. Add seasonings and stir to combine. Drain grease and let cool for about 5 minutes.
2. To assemble the salad, place all ingredients into a large bowl. Toss to mix then add dressing and toss. Top with reduced-fat sour cream and/or salsa if desired.

Nutrition Facts Per Serving

Calories 449 Total Carbs 9g Net Carbs 4g Protein 40g Fat 22g Sugar 3g Fiber 5g

Blue Apple & Cranberry Salad

Total time: 15 minutes, Serves: 10

Ingredients:

12 oz. salad greens
3 Honeycrisp apples, sliced thin
½ lemon
½ cup blue cheese, crumbled
What you'll need from store cupboard:
Apple Cider Vinaigrette (chapter 13)
1 cup pecan halves, toasted
¾ cup dried cranberries

Instructions:

1. Put the apple slices in a large plastic bag and squeeze the half lemon over them. Close the bag and shake to coat.
2. In a large bowl, layer greens, apples, pecans, cranberries, and blue cheese. Just before serving, drizzle with enough vinaigrette to dress the salad. Toss to coat all ingredients evenly.

Nutrition Facts Per Serving

Calories 291 Total Carbs 19g Net Carbs 15g Protein 5g Fat 23g Sugar 13g Fiber 4g

Pecan Pear Salad with Cranberries

Total time: 15 minutes, Serves: 8

Ingredients:

10 oz. mixed greens
3 pears, chopped
½ cup blue cheese, crumbled
What you'll need from store cupboard:
2 cups pecan halves
1 cup dried cranberries
½ cup olive oil
6 tbsps. champagne vinegar
2 tbsps. Dijon mustard
¼ tsp. salt

Instructions:

1. In a large bowl combine greens, pears, cranberries and pecans.
2. Whisk remaining ingredients, except blue cheese, together in a small bowl. Pour over salad and toss to coat. Serve topped with blue cheese crumbles.

Nutrition Facts Per Serving

Calories 325 Total Carbs 20g Net Carbs 14g Protein 5g Fat 26g Sugar 10g Fiber 6g

Walnut Portobello Salad

Prep time: 5 minutes, Cook time: 10 minutes, Serves: 4

Ingredients:

6 cups mixed salad greens
1 cup Portobello mushrooms, sliced
1 green onion, sliced
What you'll need from store cupboard:
Dijon Walnut Vinaigrette (chapter 13)
1 tbsp. olive oil
⅛ tsp. ground black pepper

Instructions:

1. Heat oil in a nonstick skillet over med-high heat. Add mushrooms and cook, stirring occasionally, 10 minutes, or until they are tender. Stir in onions and reduce heat to low.
2. Place salad greens on serving plates, top with mushrooms and sprinkle with pepper. Drizzle lightly with your choice of vinaigrette.

Nutrition Facts Per Serving

Calories 81 Total Carbs 9g Net Carbs 7g Protein 4g Fat 4g Sugar 0g Fiber 0g

Mayonnaise Chicken Salad

Prep time: 10 minutes, Serves: 6

Ingredients:

2 cups chicken, cooked and shredded
1 small red bell pepper, diced fine
¼ cup red onion, diced fine
What you'll need from store cupboard:
¼ cup reduced-fat mayonnaise
1½ tsps. ground cumin
1 tsp. garlic powder
½ tsps. coriander
Salt and pepper to taste

Instructions:

1. Combine all ingredients in a large bowl and mix to thoroughly combine. Taste and adjust seasonings as desired. Cover and chill until ready to serve.

Nutrition Facts Per Serving

Calories 117 Total Carbs 4g Net Carbs 0g Protein 14g Fat 5g Sugar 2g Fiber 0g

Quick Pickled Cucumber & Onion Salad

Total time: 10 minutes, Serves: 2

Ingredients:

½ cucumber, peeled and sliced
¼ cup red onion, sliced thin
What you'll need from store cupboard:
1 tbsp. olive oil
1 tbsp. white vinegar
1 tsp. dill

Instructions:

1. Place all ingredients in a medium bowl and toss to combine. Serve.

Nutrition Facts Per Serving

Calories 79 Total Carbs 4g Net Carbs 3g Protein 1g Fat 7g Sugar 2g Fiber 1g

Baked Salmon with Mayonnaise , page 29

Spicy Coconut Shrimp , page 29

Cajun Flounder and Tomatoes , page 29

Baked Flounder with Green Beans , page 30

Chapter 6 Fish and Seafood Recipe

Baked Salmon with Mayonnaise

Prep time: 5 minutes, Cook time: 20 minutes, Serves: 4

Ingredients:
1 lb. wild caught salmon fillets
2 tbsps. nut butter
What you'll need from store cupboard:
¼ cup reduced fat parmesan cheese, grated
¼ cup light mayonnaise
2-3 cloves garlic, diced
2 tbsps. parsley
Salt and pepper

Instructions:
1. Heat oven to 350 °F and line a baking pan with parchment paper.
2. Place salmon on pan and season with salt and pepper.
3. In a medium skillet, over medium heat, melt butter. Add garlic and cook, stirring 1 minute.
4. Reduce heat to low and add remaining ingredients. Stir until everything is melted and combined.
5. Spread evenly over salmon and bake 15 minutes for thawed fish or 20 for frozen. Salmon is done when it flakes easily with a fork. Serve.

Nutrition Facts Per Serving

Calories 408 Total Carbs 4g Net Carbs 3g Protein 41g Fat 24g Sugar 1g Fiber 0g

Cajun Flounder and Tomatoes

Prep time: 10 minutes, Cook time: 15 minutes, Serves: 4

Ingredients:
4 flounder fillets
2½ cups tomatoes, diced
¾ cup onion, diced
¾ cup green bell pepper, diced
What you'll need from store cupboard:
2 cloves garlic, diced fine
1 tbsp. Cajun seasoning
1 tsp. olive oil

Instructions:
1. Heat oil in a large skillet over med-high heat. Add onion and garlic and cook 2 minutes, or until soft. Add tomatoes, peppers and spices, and cook 2-3 minutes until tomatoes soften.
2. Lay fish over top. Cover, reduce heat to medium and cook, 5-8 minutes, or until fish flakes easily with a fork. Transfer fish to serving plates and top with sauce.

Nutrition Facts Per Serving

Calories 194 Total Carbs 8g Net Carbs 6g Protein 32g Fat 3g Sugar 5g Fiber 2g

Spicy Coconut Shrimp

Prep time: 15 minutes, Cook time: 20 minutes, Serves: 6

Ingredients:
2 lbs. jumbo shrimp, peel & devein & pat dry
2 eggs
What you'll need from store cupboard:
¾ cup unsweetened coconut
¾ cup coconut flour
½ cup sunflower oil
1 tbsp. Creole seasoning
2 tsps. Splenda
1 tsp. salt
½ tsp. garlic powder
Sriracha Mayo Dipping Sauce, (chapter 13)

Instructions:
1. Heat oil in a pot over med-high heat, you need about 3 inches of oil.
2. In a medium bowl, combine coconut, flour, Creole seasoning, salt, garlic powder, and Splenda.
3. In a small bowl beat the eggs.
4. Dip shrimp in the eggs then the coconut mixture to coat. Cook, ⅓ of the shrimp at a time, 2-3 minutes, or until golden brown. Transfer to paper towel lined plate.
5. Serve hot with Sriracha Mayo Dipping Sauce, or your favorite dipping sauce.

Nutrition Facts Per Serving

Calories 316 Total Carbs 10g Net Carbs 7g Protein 29g Fat 17g Sugar 6g Fiber 3g

Baked Flounder with Green Beans

Prep time: 10 minutes, Cook time: 20 minutes, serves 4

Ingredients:

1 lb. flounder fillets
2 cups green beans
4 tbsps. nut butter
8 basil leaves
What you'll need from store cupboard:
1¾ oz. pork rinds
½ cup reduced fat parmesan cheese
3 cloves garlic
Salt and pepper to taste
Nonstick cooking spray

Instructions:

1. Heat oven to 350 °F. Spray a baking dish with cooking spray.
2. Steam green beans until they are almost tender, about 15 minutes, less if you use frozen or canned beans. Lay green beans in the prepared dish.
3. Place the fish fillets over the green beans and season with salt and pepper.
4. Place the garlic, basil, pork rinds, and parmesan in a food processor and pulse until mixture resembles crumbs. Sprinkle over fish. Cut nut butter into small pieces and place on top.
5. Bake 15-20 minutes or until fish flakes easily with a fork. Serve.

Nutrition Facts Per Serving

Calories 358 Total Carbs 5g Net Carbs 4g Protein 39g Fat 20g Sugar 1g Fiber 2g

Cajun Roasted Shrimp and Vegetables

Prep time: 5 minutes, Cook time: 15 minutes, Serves: 4

Ingredients:

1 lb. large shrimp, peeled and deveined
2 zucchinis, sliced
2 yellow squash, sliced
½ bunch asparagus, cut into thirds
2 red bell pepper, cut into chunks
What you'll need from store cupboard:
2 tbsps. olive oil
2 tbsps. Cajun Seasoning
Salt & pepper, to taste

Instructions:

1. Heat oven to 400 °F.
2. Combine shrimp and vegetables in a large bowl. Add oil and seasoning and toss to coat.
3. Spread evenly in a large baking sheet and bake 15-20 minutes, or until vegetables are tender. Serve.

Nutrition Facts Per Serving

Calories 251 Total Carbs 13g Net Carbs 9g Protein 30g Fat 9g Sugar 6g Fiber 4g

Chili Catfish

Prep time: 5 minutes, Cook time: 15 minutes, Serves: 4

Ingredients:

4 (8 oz.) catfish fillets
What you'll need from store cupboard:
2 tbsps. olive oil
2 tsps. garlic salt
2 tsps. thyme
2 tsps. paprika
½ tsp. cayenne pepper
½ tsp. red hot sauce
¼ tsp. black pepper
Nonstick cooking spray

Instructions:

1. Heat oven to 450 °F. Spray a 9x13-inch baking dish with cooking spray.
2. In a small bowl whisk together everything but catfish. Brush both sides of fillets, using all the spice mix.
3. Bake 10-13 minutes or until fish flakes easily with a fork. Serve.

Nutrition Facts Per Serving

Calories 366 Total Carbs 0g Net Carbs 0g Protein 35g Fat 24g Sugar 0g Fiber 0g

Crab & Onion Frittata

Prep time: 10 minutes, Cook time: 50 minutes, Serves: 4

Ingredients:

4 eggs
2 cups lump crabmeat
1 cup nonfat half-n-half
1 cup green onions, diced
What you'll need from store cupboard:
1 cup reduced fat parmesan cheese, grated
1 tsp. salt
1 tsp. pepper
1 tsp. smoked paprika
1 tsp. Italian seasoning
Nonstick cooking spray

Instructions:

1. Heat oven to 350 °F. Spray an 8-inch springform pan, or pie plate with cooking spray.
2. In a large bowl, whisk together the eggs and half-n-half. Add seasonings and parmesan cheese, stir to mix.
3. Stir in the onions and crab meat. Pour into prepared pan and bake 35-40 minutes, or eggs are set and top is lightly browned.
4. Let cool 10 minutes, then slice and serve warm or at room temperature.

Nutrition Facts Per Serving

Calories 276 Total Carbs 5g Net Carbs 4g Protein 25g Fat 17g Sugar 1g Fiber 1g

Spicy Fish & Tomatoes

Prep time: 10 minutes, Cook time: 2 hours 30 minutes, Serves: 4

Ingredients:

1 lb. cod fillets
1 bell pepper, diced
1 small onion, diced
What you'll need from store cupboard:
15 oz. can tomatoes, diced
⅓ cup low-sodium vegetable broth
1 clove garlic, diced fine
½ tsp. basil
½ tsp. oregano
½ tsp. salt
¼ tsp. pepper

Instructions:

1. Place the onion, bell pepper, tomatoes, and garlic in the crock pot. Stir to mix.
2. Place fish on top. Sprinkle with herbs and seasonings. Pour broth over top.
3. Cover and cook on high 1-2 hours, or low 2-4 hours.

Nutrition Facts Per Serving

Calories 165 Total Carbs 11g Net Carbs 8g Protein 28g Fat 1g Sugar 6g Fiber 3g

Crunchy Lemon Shrimps

Prep time: 5 minutes, Cook time: 10 minutes, Serves: 4

Ingredients:

1 lb. raw shrimp, peeled and deveined
2 tbsps. Italian parsley, roughly chopped
2 tbsps. lemon juice, divided
What you'll need from store cupboard:
⅔ cup panko bread crumbs
2½ tbsps. olive oil, divided
Salt and pepper, to taste

Instructions:

1. Heat oven to 400 °F.
2. Place the shrimp evenly in a baking dish and sprinkle with salt and pepper. Drizzle on 1 tbsp. lemon juice and 1 tbsp. of olive oil. Set aside.
3. In a medium bowl, combine parsley, remaining lemon juice, bread crumbs, remaining olive oil, and ¼ tsp. each of salt and pepper. Layer the panko mixture evenly on top of the shrimp.
4. Bake 8-10 minutes or until shrimp are cooked through and the panko is golden brown.

Nutrition Facts Per Serving

Calories 283 Total Carbs 15g Net Carbs 14g Protein 28g Fat 12g Sugar 1g Fiber 1g

Garlic Shrimps with Sun Dried Tomatoes

Prep time: 10 minutes, Cook time: 30 minutes, Serves: 4

Ingredients:

½ lb. shrimp, peeled and deveined
4 oz. sun-dried tomatoes
1 cup nonfat half-n-half
What you'll need from store cupboard:
1 cup reduced fat parmesan cheese
4 cloves garlic, diced fine
2 tbsps. olive oil
1 tsp. dried basil
¼ tsp. salt
¼ tsp. paprika
¼ tsp. crushed red pepper
½ recipe Homemade Pasta, cook and drain, (chapter 4)

Instructions:

1. Heat oil in a large skillet over medium heat. Add garlic and tomatoes and cook 1 minute.
2. Add shrimp, sprinkle with salt and paprika, and cook about 2 minutes.
3. Add half-n-half, basil, and crushed red pepper and bring to boil. Reduce heat to simmer. Whisk the parmesan cheese into the hot cream and stir to melt cheese, on low heat.
4. Remove from heat. Add pasta and stir to coat. Serve.

Nutrition Facts Per Serving

Calories 353 Total Carbs 23g Net Carbs 20g Protein 37g Fat 22g Sugar 3g Fiber 3g

Basil Grilled Tuna Steaks

Prep time: 5 minutes, Cook time: 10 minutes, Serves: 6

Ingredients:

6 (6 oz.) tuna steaks
3 tbsps. fresh basil, diced
What you'll need from store cupboard:
4½ tsps. olive oil
¾ tsp. salt
¼ tsp. pepper
Nonstick cooking spray

Instructions:

1. Heat grill to medium heat. Spray rack with cooking spray.
2. Drizzle both sides of the tuna with oil. Sprinkle with basil, salt and pepper.
3. Place on grill and cook 5 minutes per side, tuna should be slightly pink in the center. Serve.

Nutrition Facts Per Serving

Calories 343 Total Carbs 0g Net Carbs 0g Protein 51g Fat 14g Sugar 0g Fiber 0g

Italian Steamed Mussels with White Wine

Ingredients:

2 lbs. mussels, cleaned
2 plum tomatoes, peeled, seeded and diced
1 cup onion, diced
2 tbsps. fresh parsley, diced
What you'll need from store cupboard:
¼ cup dry white wine
3 cloves garlic, diced fine
3 tbsps. olive oil
2 tbsps. fresh breadcrumbs
¼ tsp. crushed red pepper flakes

Instructions:

1. Heat oil in a large sauce pot over medium heat. Add the onions and cook until soft, about 2-3 minutes. Add garlic and cook 1 minute more.
2. Stir in wine, tomatoes, and pepper flakes. Bring to a boil, stirring occasionally. Add the mussels and cook 3-4 minutes, or until all the mussels have opened. Discard any mussels that do not open.
3. Once mussels open, transfer them to a serving bowl. Add bread crumbs to the sauce and continue to cook, stirring frequently, until mixture thickens. Stir in parsley and pour evenly over mussels. Serve.

Nutrition Facts Per Serving

Calories 340 Total Carbs 18g Net Carbs 16g Protein 29g Fat 16g Sugar 4g Fiber 2g

Chili Maple Glazed Salmon

Ingredients:

3 lbs. salmon fillets
What you'll need from store cupboard:
½ cup sugar free maple syrup
3 tbsps. Dijon mustard
2 tbsps. chili powder
2 tbsps. paprika
1½ tbsps. Splenda
1½ tsps. salt

Instructions:

1. Heat oven to 375 °F. Line a large baking sheet with foil, you need enough to fold foil, and seal over the fish.
2. In a small bowl, stir together mustard, chili powder, smoked paprika, Splenda, and salt.
3. Place the salmon on the foil and using the back of a spoon, spread with the mustard paste.
4. Pull the foil up and over the salmon, being careful to not lay the foil on the salmon as the paste will stick to it, and pinch the foil closed like a packet.

5. Bake for 14-15 minutes. Remove from the oven and carefully open the foil, avoiding the escaping steam.
6. Turn oven to broil. Drizzle the salmon with the maple syrup. Broil 2-3 minutes. Serve.

Nutrition Facts Per Serving

Calories 248 Total Carbs 4g Net Carbs 3g Protein 33g Fat 11g Sugar 2g Fiber 1g

Garlic Maple Salmon

Ingredients:

1½ lbs. salmon fillets
1 tbsp. orange juice
What you'll need from store cupboard:
2 tbsps. sugar free maple syrup
2 tbsps. grainy Dijon mustard
2 tsps. garlic, diced fine
Nonstick cooking spray

Instructions:

1. Heat oven to 375 °F. Spray baking dish with cooking spray and lay salmon in dish, skin side down.
2. In a small mixing bowl, whisk together orange juice, syrup, mustard, and garlic. Pour sauce over fish and cover with foil.
3. Bake 15 minutes. Uncover, and bake another 5 minutes until top of fish is caramelized and fish flakes easily with a fork.

Nutrition Facts Per Serving

Calories 247 Total Carbs 6g Net Carbs 5g Protein 33g Fat 11g Sugar 1g Fiber 0g

Pan Seared Trout with Lemon

Ingredients:

6 (6 oz.) trout fillets
6 lemon slices
What you'll need from store cupboard:
4 tbsps. olive oil
¾ tsp. salt
½ tsp. pepper
Italian-Style Salsa, (chapter 13)

Instructions:

1. Sprinkle fillets with salt and pepper.
2. Heat oil in a large nonstick skillet over med-high heat. Cook trout, 3 fillets at a time, 2-3 minutes per side, or fish flakes easily with a fork. Repeat with remaining fillets.
3. Serve topped with salsa and a slice of lemon.

Nutrition Facts Per Serving

Calories 320 Total Carbs 2g Net Carbs 1g Protein 30g Fat 21g Sugar 1g Fiber 0g

Tomato Clam Sauce & Pasta

Prep time: 10 minutes, Cook time: 3 hours, Serves: 4

Ingredients:

1 onion, diced
¼ cup fresh parsley, diced
What you'll need from store cupboard:
2 (6½ oz.) cans clams, chopped, undrained
14½ oz. tomatoes, diced, undrained
6 oz. tomato paste
2 cloves garlic, diced
1 bay leaf
1 tbsp. sunflower oil
1 tsp. Splenda
1 tsp. basil
½ tsp. thyme
½ recipe Homemade Pasta, cook & drain (chapter 4)

Instructions:

1. Heat oil in a small skillet over med-high heat. Add onion and cook until tender, Add garlic and cook 1 minute more. Transfer to crock pot.
2. Add remaining ingredients, except pasta, cover and cook on low 3-4 hours.
3. Discard bay leaf and serve over cooked pasta.

Nutrition Facts Per Serving

Calories 223 Total Carbs 32g Net Carbs 27g Protein 12g Fat 6g Sugar 15g Fiber 5g

Salmon with Basil Pesto

Prep time: 10 minutes, Cook time: 20 minutes, Serves: 6

Ingredients:

2½ lbs. salmon fillets
2 tomatoes, sliced
½ cup nut butter
What you'll need from store cupboard:
½ cup basil pesto

Instructions:

1. Heat the oven to 400 °F. Line a 9x15-inch baking sheet with foil, making sure it covers the sides. Place another large piece of foil onto the baking sheet and place the salmon fillets on top of it.
2. Place the pesto and nut butter in blender or food processor and pulse until smooth. Spread evenly over salmon. Place tomato slices on top.
3. Wrap the foil around the salmon, tenting around the top to prevent foil from touching the salmon as much as possible. Bake 15-25 minutes, or salmon flakes easily with a fork. Serve.

Nutrition Facts Per Serving

Calories 444 Total Carbs 2g Net Carbs 1g Protein 55g Fat 24g Sugar 1g Fiber 0g

Mozzarella Chicken & Spinach, page 35

Chicken Spinach Tuscany, page 35

Chicken Mushroom Marsala, page 35

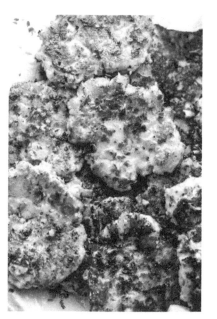

Chicken Zucchini Patties with Mayonnaise, page 36

Mozzarella Chicken & Spinach

Prep time: 10 minutes, Cook time: 45 minutes, Serves: 6

Ingredients:

3 chicken breasts, boneless, skinless and halved lengthwise
6 oz. low fat cream cheese, soft
2 cups baby spinach
1 cup mozzarella cheese, grated
What you'll need from store cupboard:
2 tbsps. olive oil, divided
3 cloves garlic, diced fine
1 tsp. Italian seasoning
Nonstick cooking spray

Instructions:

1. Heat oven to 350 °F. Spray a 9x13-inch glass baking dish with cooking spray.
2. Lay chicken breast cutlets in baking dish. Drizzle 1 tbsp. oil over chicken. Sprinkle evenly with garlic and Italian seasoning. Spread cream cheese over the top of chicken.
3. Heat remaining tbsp. of oil in a small skillet over medium heat. Add spinach and cook until spinach wilts, about 3 minutes. Place evenly over cream cheese layer. Sprinkle mozzarella over top.
4. Bake 35-40 minutes, or until chicken is cooked through. Serve.

Nutrition Facts Per Serving

Calories 363 Total Carbs 3g Net Carbs 2g Protein 31g Fat 25g Sugar 0g Fiber 0g

Chicken Mushroom Marsala

Prep time: 10 minutes, Cook time: 25 minutes, Serves: 4

Ingredients:

4 boneless chicken breasts
½ lb. mushrooms, sliced
1 tbsp. nut butter
What you'll need from store cupboard:
1 cup Marsala wine
¼ cup flour
1 tbsp. oil
Pinch of white pepper
Pinch of oregano
Pinch of basil

Instructions:

1. On a shallow plate, combine flour and seasonings.
2. Dredge the chicken in the flour mixture to coat both sides.

3. In a large skillet, over medium heat, heat oil until hot. Add chicken and cook until brown on both sides, about 15 minutes. Transfer chicken to a plate.
4. Reduce heat to low and add mushrooms and ¼ cup of the wine. Cook about 5 minutes. Scrape bottom of pan to loosen any flour. Stir in reserved flour mixture and the remaining wine.
5. Simmer until mixture starts to thicken, stirring constantly. Add the chicken back to the pan and cook an additional 5 minutes. Serve.

Nutrition Facts Per Serving

Calories 327 Total Carbs 9g Net Carbs 8g Protein 21g Fat 14g Sugar 1g Fiber 1g

Chicken Spinach Tuscany

Prep time: 10 minutes, Cook time: 15 minutes, Serves: 4

Ingredients:

1½ lbs. chicken breasts, boneless, skinless and sliced thin
1 cup spinach, chopped
1 cup nonfat half-n-half
What you'll need from store cupboard:
½ cup reduced fat parmesan cheese
½ cup low sodium chicken broth
½ cup sun dried tomatoes
2 tbsps. olive oil
1 tsp. Italian seasoning
1 tsp. garlic powder

Instructions:

1. Heat oil in a large skillet over med-high heat. Add chicken and cook 3-5 minutes per side, or until browned and cooked through. Transfer to a plate.
2. Add half-n-half, broth, cheese and seasonings to the pan. Whisk constantly until sauce starts to thicken. Add spinach and tomatoes and cook, stirring frequently, until spinach starts to wilt, about 2-3 minutes.
3. Add chicken back to the pan and cook just long enough to heat through.

Nutrition Facts Per Serving

Calories 462 Total Carbs 6g Net Carbs 5g Protein 55g Fat 23g Sugar 0g Fiber 1g

Chicken Zucchini Patties with Mayonnaise

Prep time: 10 minutes, Cook time: 10 minutes, Serves: 8

Ingredients:

2 cups chicken breast, cooked, divided
1 zucchini, cut in ¾-inch pieces
¼ cup cilantro, diced

What you'll need from store cupboard:

⅓ cup bread crumbs
⅓ cup lite mayonnaise
2 tsps. olive oil
½ tsp. salt
¼ tsp. pepper
Roasted Tomato Salsa, (chapter 13)

Instructions:

1. Place 1½ cups chicken and zucchini into a food processor. Cover and process until coarsely chopped. Add bread crumbs, mayonnaise, pepper, cilantro, remaining chicken, and salt. Cover and pulse until chunky.
2. Heat oil in a large skillet over med-high heat. Shape chicken mixture into 8 patties and cook 4 minutes per side, or until golden brown. Serve topped with salsa.

Nutrition Facts Per Serving

Calories 146 Total Carbs 10g Net Carbs 8g Protein 12g Fat 7g Sugar 5g Fiber 2g

Chili Chicken Tenders

Prep time: 5 minutes, Cook time: 15 minutes, Serves: 4

Ingredients:

1 lb. chicken breast tenders
1 cup nonfat half-n-half
4 tbsps. nut butter

What you'll need from store cupboard:

2 tsps. garlic powder
2 tsps. chili powder

Instructions:

1. In a small bowl, stir together seasonings with a little salt if desired. Sprinkle over chicken to coat.
2. Heat 2 tbsps. nut butter in a large skillet over medium heat. Cook chicken until no longer pink, 3-4 minutes per side. Transfer to a plate.
3. Add half-n-half and stir, scraping up the brown bits from the bottom of the skillet, and cook until it starts to boil. Reduce heat to med-low and simmer until sauce is reduced by half. Stir in remaining nut butter and add chicken back to sauce to heat through. Serve.

Nutrition Facts Per Serving

Calories 281 Total Carbs 3g Net Carbs 2g Protein 24g Fat 19g Sugar 0g Fiber 0g

Roasted Duck Legs

Prep time: 10 minutes, Cook time: 90 minutes, Serves: 4

Ingredients:

4 duck legs
3 plum tomatoes, diced
1 red chili, deseeded and sliced
½ small Savoy cabbage, quartered
2 tsps. fresh ginger, grated

What you'll need from store cupboard:

3 cloves garlic, sliced
2 tbsps. soy sauce
1 drop liquid stevia
1 tsp. five-spice powder

Instructions:

1. Heat oven to 350 °F.
2. Place the duck in a large skillet over low heat and cook until brown on all sides and most of the fat is rendered, about 10 minutes. Transfer duck to a deep baking dish. Drain off all but 2 tbsps. of the fat.
3. Add ginger, garlic, and chili to the skillet and cook 2 minutes until soft. Add soy sauce, tomatoes and 2 tbsps. water and bring to a boil.
4. Rub the duck with the five spice seasoning. Pour the sauce over the duck and drizzle with the liquid stevia. Cover with foil and bake 1 hour. Add the cabbage for the last 10 minutes.

Nutrition Facts Per Serving

Calories 211 Total Carbs 19g Net Carbs 16g Protein 25g Fat 5g Sugar 14g Fiber 3g

Garlic Chicken Thighs

Prep time: 5 minutes, Cook time: 6 hours, Serves: 6

Ingredients:

6 chicken thighs

What you'll need from store cupboard:

2 tbsps. sugar free ketchup
¼ tsp. stevia extract
2 tbsps. lite soy sauce
3 cloves garlic, diced fine

Instructions:

1. Add everything, except chicken, to the crock pot. Stir to combine.
2. Lay chicken, skin side up, in a single layer. Cover and cook on low 6 hours, or high for 3 hours.
3. Place chicken in a baking dish and broil 2-3 minutes to caramelize the outside. Serve.

Nutrition Facts Per Serving

Calories 57 Total Carbs 7g Net Carbs 5g Protein 4g Fat 2g Sugar 6g Fiber 0g

Chutney Turkey and Spinach Burgers

Prep time: 10 minutes, Cook time: 15 minutes, Serves: 4

Ingredients:

1 lb. lean ground turkey
16 baby spinach leaves
4 slices red onion
2 green onions, diced
½ cup chutney, divided
¼ cup fresh parsley, diced
2 tsps. lime juice

What you'll need from store cupboard:

8 Flourless Burger Buns, (chapter 4)
1 tbsp. Dijon mustard
½ tsp. salt
¼ tsp. pepper
Nonstick cooking spray

Instructions:

1. Heat grill to med-high heat. Spray rack with cooking spray.
2. In a small bowl, combine ¼ cup chutney, mustard, and lime juice.
3. In a large bowl, combine parsley, green onions, salt, pepper, and remaining chutney. Crumble turkey over mixture and mix well. Shape into 4 patties.
4. Place burgers on the grill and cook 5-7 minutes per side, or meat thermometer reaches 165 °F.
5. Serve on buns with spinach leaves, sliced onions and reserved chutney mixture.

Nutrition Facts Per Serving

Calories 275 Total Carbs 15g Net Carbs 13g Protein 28g Fat 11g Sugar 2g Fiber 2g

Creole Chicken with Cauliflower Rice

Prep time: 15 minutes, Cook time: 25 minutes, Serves: 2

Ingredients:

2 chicken breast halves, boneless and skinless
1 cup cauliflower rice, cooked
⅓ cup green bell pepper, julienned
¼ cup celery, diced
¼ cup onion, diced

What you'll need from store cupboard:

14½ oz. stewed tomatoes, diced
1 tsp. sunflower oil
1 tsp. chili powder
½ tsp. thyme
⅛ tsp. pepper

Instructions:

1. Heat oil in a small skillet over medium heat. Add chicken and cook 5-6 minutes per side or cooked through. Transfer to plate and keep warm.
2. Add the pepper, celery, onion, tomatoes, and seasonings. Bring to a boil. Reduce heat, cover, and simmer 10 minutes or until vegetables start to soften.
3. Add chicken back to pan to heat through. Serve over cauliflower rice.

Nutrition Facts Per Serving

Calories 362 Total Carbs 14g Net Carbs 10g Protein 45g Fat 14g Sugar 8g Fiber 4g

Curried Chicken and Apples

Prep time: 15 minutes, Cook time: 30 minutes, Serves: 4

Ingredients:

1 lb. chicken breasts, boneless, skinless, cut in 1-inch cubes
2 tart apples, peel and slice
1 sweet onion, cut in half and slice
1 jalapeno, seeded and diced
2 tbsps. cilantro, diced
½ tsp. ginger, grated

What you'll need from store cupboard:

14½ oz. tomatoes, diced and drained
½ cup water
3 cloves garlic, diced
2 tbsps. sunflower oil
1 tsp. salt
1 tsp. coriander
½ tsp. turmeric
¼ tsp. cayenne pepper

Instructions:

1. Heat oil in a large skillet over med-high heat. Add chicken and onion, and cook until onion is tender. Add garlic and cook 1 more minute.
2. Add apples, water and seasonings and stir to combine. Bring to a boil. Reduce heat and simmer 12-15 minutes, or until chicken is cooked through, stirring occasionally.
3. Stir in tomatoes, jalapeno, and cilantro and serve.

Nutrition Facts Per Serving

Calories 371 Total Carbs 23g Net Carbs 18g Protein 34g Fat 16g Sugar 15g Fiber 5g

Crunchy Lemon Grilled Chicken

Prep time: 15 minutes, Cook time: 10 minutes, Serves: 8

Ingredients:

8 chicken breast halves, boneless and skinless
1 cup fat free sour cream
¼ cup lemon juice
Butter flavored spray, refrigerated
What you'll need from store cupboard:
2 cups stuffing mix, crushed
4 tsps. Worcestershire sauce
2 tsps. paprika
1 tsp. celery salt
⅛ tsp. garlic powder
Nonstick cooking spray

Instructions:

1. In a large Ziploc bag combine sour cream, lemon juice, Worcestershire, and seasonings. Add chicken, seal, and turn to coat. Refrigerate 1-4 hours.
2. Heat grill to medium heat. Spray rack with cooking spray.
3. Place stuffing crumbs in a shallow dish. Coat both sides of chicken with crumbs and spritz with butter spray.
4. Place on grill and cook 4-7 minutes per side, or until chicken is cooked through. Serve.

Nutrition Facts Per Serving

Calories 230 Total Carbs 22g Net Carbs 21g Protein 25g Fat 3g Sugar 4g Fiber 1g

Turkey and Mushroom Stuffed Peppers

Prep time: 10 minutes, Cook time: 55 minutes, Serves: 8

Ingredients:

1 lb. lean ground turkey
4 green bell peppers, halved and ribs and seeds removed
1 onion, diced
1½ cups mozzarella cheese
1 cup cauliflower, grated
1 cup mushrooms, diced
What you'll need from store cupboard:
3 cups spaghetti sauce
3 cloves garlic, diced fine
2 tbsps. olive oil

Instructions:

1. Heat the oil in a large skillet over med-high heat. Add the garlic, mushrooms, and onion. Add the turkey, cook, breaking up the turkey with a spatula, until turkey is cooked through, about 10 minutes.
2. Stir in the cauliflower, and cook, stirring frequently, 3-5 minutes. Add the spaghetti sauce and 1 cup mozzarella. Stir to combine and remove from heat.

3. Heat oven to 350 °F. Place bell peppers in a large baking dish, skin side down. Fill the insides with the turkey mixture, place any extra filling around the peppers. Top each pepper with remaining mozzarella. Bake 40-45 minutes or the peppers are tender. Serve immediately.

Nutrition Facts Per Serving

Calories 214 Total Carbs 14g Net Carbs 10g Protein 20g Fat 11g Sugar 9g Fiber 4g

Cheesy Chicken Salad Casserole

Prep time: 15 minutes, Cook time: 30 minutes, Serves: 6

Ingredients:

3 cups chicken breast, cooked and cut into cubes
6 oz. container plain low-fat yogurt
1 cup celery, diced
1 cup yellow or red sweet pepper, diced
¾ cup cheddar cheese, grated
¼ cup green onions, diced
What you'll need from store cupboard:
1 can reduced-fat and reduced-sodium condensed cream of chicken soup
½ cup cornflakes, crushed
¼ cup almonds, sliced
1 tbsp. lemon juice
¼ tsp. ground black pepper

Instructions:

1. Heat oven to 400 °F.
2. In a large bowl, combine chicken, celery, red pepper, cheese, soup, yogurt, onions, lemon juice, and black pepper, stir to combine. Transfer to 2-quart baking dish.
3. In a small bowl stir the cornflakes and almonds together. Sprinkle evenly over chicken mixture.
4. Bake 30 minutes or until heated through. Let rest 10 minutes before serving.

Nutrition Facts Per Serving

Calories 238 Total Carbs 9g Net Carbs 8g Protein 27g Fat 10g Sugar 3g Fiber 1g

Korean Chili Chicken

Ingredients:
2 lbs. chicken thighs, boneless and skinless
2 tbsps. fresh ginger, grated
What you'll need from store cupboard:
4 cloves garlic, diced fine
¼ cup lite soy sauce
2 drops liquid stevia
2 tbsps. Korean chili paste
2 tbsps. toasted sesame oil
2 tsps. cornstarch
Pinch of red pepper flakes

Instructions:
1. Add the soy sauce, liquid stevia, chili paste, sesame oil, ginger, garlic and pepper flakes to the crock pot, stir to combine. Add the chicken and turn to coat in the sauce.
2. Cover and cook on low 3-4 hours or till chicken is cooked through.
3. When the chicken is cooked, transfer it to a plate.
4. Pour the sauce into a medium saucepan. Whisk the cornstarch and ¼ cup cold water until smooth. Add it to the sauce. Cook over medium heat, stirring constantly, about 5 minutes, or until sauce is thick and glossy.
5. Use 2 forks and shred the chicken. Add it to the sauce and stir to coat. Serve.

Nutrition Facts Per Serving

Calories 397 Total Carbs 18g Net Carbs 15g Protein 44g Fat 16g Sugar 13g Fiber 0g

Mediterranean Grilled Chicken Breasts

Prep time: 5 minutes, Cook time: 10 minutes, Serves: 4

Ingredients:
4 chicken breasts, boneless, skinless
What you'll need from store cupboard:
6 oz. pesto
¼ cup olive oil
¼ cup lemon juice
2 tbsps. red wine vinegar
2 tsps. garlic, diced fine

Instructions:
1. In a large freezer bag or a container mix together the olive oil, lemon juice, red wine vinegar, minced garlic and pesto. Add chicken and toss to coat. Place in refrigerator and marinate for 6 to 8 hours.
2. Heat grill to med-high. Cook chicken, 3-4 minutes per side, or until cooked through. Or, you can bake it in a 400 degree oven until no longer pink, about 30 minutes. Serve.

Nutrition Facts Per Serving

Calories 378 Total Carbs 2g Net Carbs 1g Protein 36g Fat 25g Sugar 2g Fiber 0g

Lemon Chicken & Peppers

Prep time: 10 minutes, Cook time: 10 minutes, Serves: 4

Ingredients:
3 large boneless, skinless chicken breasts, cut into strips
¼ cup red bell pepper, cut into 2 inch strips
¼ cup green bell pepper, cut into 2 inch strips
¼ cup snow peas
¼ cup fresh lemon juice
1 tsp. fresh ginger, peeled and diced fine
What you'll need from store cupboard:
¼ cup + 1 tbsp. low sodium soy sauce, divided
¼ cup low-fat, low-sodium chicken broth
1 tbsp. Splenda
1 tbsp. vegetable oil
2 cloves garlic, diced fine
2 tsps. cornstarch

Instructions:
1. In a medium bowl, whisk together 1 tsp. cornstarch and 1 tbsp. soy sauce. Add chicken, cover and chill about 10 minutes.
2. In a separate medium mixing bowl, stir together lemon juice, ¼ cup soy sauce, broth, ginger, garlic, Splenda, and remaining cornstarch until thoroughly combined.
3. Heat oil in a large skillet over med-high heat. Add chicken and cook, stirring frequently, 3-4 minutes or just until chicken is no longer pink.
4. Add sauce, peppers and peas. Cook 2 more minutes or until sauce thickens and vegetables are tender-crisp. Serve.

Nutrition Facts Per Serving

Calories 242 Total Carbs 9g Net Carbs 8g Protein 27g Fat 10g Sugar 5g Fiber 1g

BBQ Pork Tacos with Cabbages，page 41

Cajun Smothered Pork Chops with Mushroom，page 41

Beef Picadillo with Green Olives，page 41

Chili Braised Oxtails，page 42

Chapter 8 Pork, Lamb and Beef Recipe

BBQ Pork Tacos with Cabbages

Prep time: 20 minutes, Cook time: 6 hours, Serves: 16

Ingredients:

2 lbs. pork shoulder, trim off excess fat
2 onions, diced fine
2 cups cabbages, shredded
What you'll need from store cupboard:
16 (6-inch) low carb whole wheat tortillas
4 chipotle peppers in adobo sauce, pureed
1 cup light barbecue sauce
2 cloves garlic, diced fine
1½ tsps. paprika

Instructions:

1. In a medium bowl, whisk together garlic, barbecue sauce and chipotles, cover and chill.
2. Place pork in the crock pot. Cover and cook on low 8-10 hours, or on high 4-6 hours.
3. Transfer pork to a cutting board. Use two forks and shred the pork, discarding the fat. Place pork back in the crock pot. Sprinkle with paprika then pour the barbecue sauce over mixture.
4. Stir to combine, cover and cook 1 hour. Skim off excess fat.
5. To assemble the tacos: place about ¼ cup of pork on warmed tortilla. Top with cabbage and onions and serve. Refrigerate any leftover pork up to 3 days.

Nutrition Facts Per Serving

Calories 265 Total Carbs 14g Net Carbs 5g Protein 17g Fat 14g Sugar 3g Fiber 9g

Beef Picadillo with Green Olives

Prep time: 10 minutes, Cook time: 3-4 hours, Serves: 10

Ingredients:

1½ lbs. lean ground beef
1 onion, diced fine
1 red bell pepper, diced
1 small tomato, diced
¼ cup cilantro, diced fine
What you'll need from store cupboard:
1 cup tomato sauce
3 cloves garlic, diced fine
¼ cup green olives, pitted
2 bay leaves
1½ tsps. cumin
¼ tsp. garlic powder
Salt & pepper, to taste

Instructions:

1. In a large skillet, over medium heat, brown ground beef. Season with salt and pepper. Drain fat. Add onion, bell pepper, and garlic and cook 3-4 minutes.
2. Transfer to crock pot and add remaining ingredients. Cover and cook on high 3 hours.
3. Discard bay leaves. Taste and adjust seasonings as desired. Serve.

Nutrition Facts Per Serving

Calories 255 Total Carbs 6g Net Carbs 5g Protein 35g Fat 9g Sugar 3g Fiber 1g

Cajun Smothered Pork Chops with Mushroom

Prep time: 5 minutes, Cook time: 25 minutes, Serves: 4

Ingredients:

4 pork chops, thick-cut
1 small onion, diced fine
1 cup mushrooms, sliced
1 cup fat free sour cream
2 tbsps. nut butter
What you'll need from store cupboard:
1 cup low sodium chicken broth
3 cloves garlic, diced fine
1 tbsp. Cajun seasoning
2 bay leaves
1 tsp. smoked paprika
Salt & pepper to taste

Instructions:

1. Melt nut butter in a large skillet over medium heat. Sprinkle chops with salt and pepper and cook until nicely browned, about 5 minutes per side. Transfer to a plate.
2. Add onions and mushrooms and cook until soft, about 5 minutes. Add garlic and cook one minute more.
3. Add broth and stir to incorporate brown bits on bottom of the pan. Add a dash of salt and the bay leaves. Add pork chops back to sauce. Bring to a simmer, cover, and reduce heat. Cook 5-8 minutes, or until chops are cooked through.
4. Transfer chops to a plate and keep warm. Bring sauce to a boil and cook until it has reduced by half, stirring occasionally.
5. Reduce heat to low and whisk in sour cream, Cajun seasoning, and paprika. Cook, stirring frequently, 3 minutes. Add chops back to the sauce and heat through. Serve.

Nutrition Facts Per Serving

Calories 323 Total Carbs 13g Net Carbs 12g Protein 24g Fat 18g Sugar 5g Fiber 1g

Chili Braised Oxtails

Prep time: 10 minutes, Cook time: 4-6 hours, Serves: 6

Ingredients:
2 pounds oxtails
1 onion, diced
½ cup nonfat half-n-half
1 tsp. nut butter
What you'll need from store cupboard:
1 cup low sodium beef broth
¼ cup sake
4 cloves garlic, diced
2 tbsps. chili sauce
1 tsp. Chinese five spice
Salt & pepper

Instructions:
1. Melt the nut butter in a large skillet over med-high heat. Sprinkle oxtails with salt and pepper and cook until brown on all sides, about 3-4 minutes per side.
2. Add onion and garlic and cook another 3-5 minutes. Add the sake to deglaze the skillet and cook until liquid is reduced, 1-2 minutes.
3. Transfer mixture to the crock pot. Add the broth, chili sauce, and five spice, stir to combine. Cover and cook on low 6 hours, or high 4 hours, or until meat is tender.
4. Stir in the half-n-half and continue cooking another 30-60 minutes or sauce has thickened. Serve.

Nutrition Facts Per Serving

Calories 447 Total Carbs 4g Net Carbs 3g Protein 48g Fat 24g Sugar 1g Fiber 0g

Tomato Braised Brisket

Prep time: 10 minutes: Cook time: 8 hours, Serves: 10

Ingredients:
5 lbs. beef brisket
1 bottle of lite beer
1 onion, sliced thin
What you'll need from store cupboard:
15 oz. can tomatoes, diced
3 cloves garlic, diced fine
1 tbsp. + 1 tsp. oregano
1 tbsp. salt
1 tbsp. black pepper

Instructions:
1. Place the onion on the bottom of the crock pot. Add brisket, fat side up. Add the tomatoes, undrained and beer. Sprinkle the garlic and seasonings on the top.
2. Cover and cook on low heat 8 hours, or until beef is fork tender.

Nutrition Facts Per Serving

Calories 445 Total Carbs 4g Net Carbs 3g Protein 69g Fat 14g Sugar 2g Fiber 1g

Asian Sesame Beef Bowls

Prep time: 15 minutes, Cook time: 15 minutes, Serves: 4

Ingredients:
1 lb. lean ground beef
1 bunch green onions, sliced
¼ cup fresh ginger, grated
What you'll need from store cupboard:
Cauliflower Rice, (chapter 4)
¼ cup toasted sesame oil
5 cloves garlic, diced fine
2 tbsps. light soy sauce
2 tsps. sesame seeds

Instructions:
1. Heat oil in a large, cast iron skillet over high heat. Add all but 2 tbsps. of the green onions and cook until soft and starting to brown, about 5 minutes.
2. Add beef, and cook, breaking up with a spatula, until no longer pink. About 8 minutes.
3. Add remaining ingredients and simmer 2-3 minutes, stirring frequently. Serve over hot cauliflower rice garnished with sesame seeds and reserved green onions.

Nutrition Facts Per Serving

Calories 383 Total Carbs 24g Net Carbs 22g Protein 40g Fat 21g Sugar 11g Fiber 2g

Garlic Butter Skirt Steak

Prep time: 5 minutes, Cook time: 8 minutes, Serves: 4

Ingredients:
1 lb. skirt steak
¼ cup fresh parsley, diced, divided
5 tbsps. nut butter
What you'll need from store cupboard:
6 tsps. garlic, diced fine
1 tbsp. olive oil
Salt and pepper for taste

Instructions:
1. Cut the steak into 4 pieces. Pat dry then season both sides with salt and pepper
2. Heat oil in a large, heavy skillet over med-high heat. Add steak and sear both sides, 2-3 minutes for medium rare, until it reaches desired doneness. Transfer to plate and cover with foil to keep warm.
3. Melt the nut butter in a separate skillet over low heat. Add garlic and cook, stirring, until garlic is a light golden brown.
4. Pour the garlic mixture into a bowl and season with salt to taste. Slice the steak against the grain and place on plates. Sprinkle parsley over steak then drizzle with garlic mixture. Serve immediately.

Nutrition Facts Per Serving

Calories 365 Total Carbs 2g Net Carbs 1g Protein 31g Fat 25g Sugar 0g Fiber 0g

Crock Pot Orange Carnitas

Prep time: 10 minutes, Cook time: 6 hours, Serves: 4

Ingredients:

4 lbs. pork butt, boneless, trim the fat and cut into 2-inch cubes
1 onion, cut in half
Juice from 1 orange, reserve orange halves
2 tbsps. fresh lime juice
What you'll need from store cupboard:
2 cups water
1½ tsps. salt
1 tsp. cumin
1 tsp. oregano
2 bay leaves
¾ tsp. pepper

Instructions:

1. Place pork and orange halves in the crock pot. In a medium bowl, combine remaining ingredients and stir to combine. Pour over pork.
2. Cover and cook on high 5 hours. Pork should be tender enough to shred with a fork. If not, cook another 60 minutes.
3. Transfer pork to a bowl. Pour the sauce into a large saucepan and discard the bay leaves and orange halves.
4. Bring to a boil and cook until it thickens and resembles a syrup.
5. Use two forks to shred the pork. Add pork to the sauce and stir to coat. Serve.

Nutrition Facts Per Serving

Calories 464 Total Carbs 3g Net Carbs 2g Protein 35g Fat 35g Sugar 1g Fiber 0g

Cheesy Beef and Noodles

Prep time: 10 minutes, Cook time: 15 minutes, Serves: 4

Ingredients:

1 lb. lean ground beef
1 onion, diced
2 cups mozzarella, grated
½ cup + 2 tbsps. fresh parsley diced
What you'll need from store cupboard:
Homemade Noodles, (chapter 4)
2 tbsps. tomato paste
1 tbsp. extra-virgin olive oil
1 tbsp. Worcestershire sauce
3 cloves garlic, diced fine
1 tsp. red pepper flakes
½ tsp. pepper
Salt, to taste

Instructions:

1. Heat oil in a large skillet over med-high heat. Add beef and cook, breaking up with a spatula, about 2 minutes.
2. Reduce heat to medium and season with salt and pepper. Stir in garlic, onion, pepper flakes, Worcestershire, tomato paste, ½ cup parsley, and ½ cup water. Bring to a simmer and cook, stirring occasionally, 8 minutes.
3. Stir in noodles and cook 2 minutes more. Stir in 1 cup of cheese, sprinkle the remaining cheese over the top and cover with lid, off the heat, until cheese melts. Serve garnished with remaining parsley.

Nutrition Facts Per Serving

Calories 372 Total Carbs 7g Net Carbs 6g Protein 44g Fat 18g Sugar 3g Fiber 1g

Sirloin Strips & Cauliflower Rice

Prep time: 15 minutes, Cook time: 30 minutes, Serves: 6

Ingredients:

1½ lbs. top sirloin steak, cut in thin strips
3 cups Cauliflower Rice, cooked, (chapter 4)
2 onions, slice thin
What you'll need from store cupboard:
14½ oz. tomatoes, diced, undrained
½ cup low sodium beef broth
⅓ cup dry red wine
1 clove garlic, diced
1 bay leaf
2 tsps. olive oil, divided
1 tsp. salt
½ tsp. basil
½ tsp. thyme
¼ tsp. pepper

Instructions:

1. Sprinkle beef strips with salt and pepper.
2. Heat oil in a large skillet over medium heat. Add steak and cook, stirring frequently, just until browned. Transfer to a plate and keep warm.
3. Add remaining oil to the skillet along with the onion and cook until tender. Add the garlic and cook 1 minute more.
4. Stir in remaining ingredients, except the cauliflower, and bring to a boil. Reduce heat and simmer 10 minutes.
5. Return the steak back to the skillet and cook 2-4 minutes until heated through and tender. Discard bay leaf and serve over cauliflower rice.

Nutrition Facts Per Serving

Calories 278 Total Carbs 9g Net Carbs 6g Protein 37g Fat 9g Sugar 5g Fiber 3g

Crock Pot Juicy Beef Roast

Prep time: 15 minutes, Cook time: 5½ hours, Serves: 10

Ingredients:

3 lbs. beef sirloin tip roast
What you'll need from store cupboard:
¼ cup lite soy sauce
¼ cup water
3 tbsps. balsamic vinegar
2 tbsps. cornstarch
2 tbsps. coarse ground pepper
1 tbsp. Worcestershire sauce
2 tsps. ground mustard
1½ tsps. garlic, diced fine

Instructions:

1. Rub roast with garlic and pepper. Cut in half and place in crock pot.
2. Combine soy sauce, vinegar, Worcestershire, and mustard, pour over roast.
3. Cover and cook on low heat 5½-6 hours or until beef is tender.
4. Remove roast and keep warm. Strain juices into a small sauce pan, skim off fat. Heat over medium heat.
5. Stir water and cornstarch together until smooth. Stir into beef juices. Bring to a boil, and cook, stirring, 2 minutes or until thickened. Serve with roast.

Nutrition Facts Per Serving

Calories 264 Total Carbs 3g Net Carbs 2g Protein 37g Fat 12g Sugar 0g Fiber 0g

Hearty Beef Chili with Tomato Sauce

Prep time: 15 minutes, Cook time: 1 hour, Serves: 4

Ingredients:

1 lb. lean ground beef
1 large bell pepper, diced
1 cup onion, diced
What you'll need from store cupboard:
4 oz. can green chilies, diced
1 cup tomato sauce
1 cup low sodium beef broth
1 tbsp. tomato paste
2 cloves garlic, diced fine
2 tsps. chili powder
1 tsp. salt
1 tsp. Worcestershire
1 tsp. cumin
½ tsp. celery salt
¼ tsp. pepper

Instructions:

1. Heat a large pan over med-high heat. Add beef, onions, bell pepper and garlic and cook, stirring occasionally, until beef is no longer pink. Drain fat.
2. Add remaining ingredients and bring to a simmer. Reduce heat to med-low and simmer 30 minutes to an hour. Taste and adjust seasonings if needed. Serve.

Nutrition Facts Per Serving

Calories 355 Total Carbs 30g Net Carbs 20g Protein 40g Fat 9g Sugar 18g Fiber 10g

Cajun Beef & Cauliflower Rice Skillet

Prep time: 10 minutes, Cook time: 25 minutes, Serves: 4

Ingredients:

¾ lb. lean ground beef
2 cups cauliflower rice, cooked
1 red bell pepper, sliced thin
½ yellow onion, diced
1 stalk celery, sliced thin
1 jalapeño pepper, seeds removed and diced fine
¼ cup fresh parsley, diced
What you'll need from store cupboard:
½ cup low sodium beef broth
4 tsps. Cajun seasoning

Instructions:

1. Place beef and 1½ tsps. Cajun seasoning in a large skillet over med-high heat. Cook, breaking apart with wooden spoon, until no longer pink, about 10 minutes.
2. Add vegetables, except cauliflower, and remaining Cajun seasoning. Cook, stirring occasionally, 6-8 minutes, or until vegetables are tender.
3. Add broth and stir, scraping brown bits from the bottom of the pan. Cook 2-3 minutes until mixture has thickened. Stir in cauliflower and cook just until heated through. Remove from heat, stir in parsley and serve.

Nutrition Facts Per Serving

Calories 198 Total Carbs 8g Net Carbs 6g Protein 28g Fat 6g Sugar 4g Fiber 2g

Swedish Mushroom Beef Noodles

Prep time: 10 minutes, Cook time: 20 minutes, Serves: 4

Ingredients:

1 lb. lean ground beef
8 oz. cremini mushrooms, sliced
1 cup onion, sliced thin
½ cup sour cream
What you'll need from store cupboard:
3½ cups low sodium beef broth
1 tsp. garlic salt
1 tsp. caraway seed
Homemade Noodles, (chapter 4)
Nonstick cooking spray

Instructions:

1. Spray a large pot with cooking spray and heat over med-high heat. Add beef and cook, breaking up with spatula, 2 minutes. Add onions and mushrooms and cook until beef is browned and onions are soft.
2. Add the garlic salt, caraway seeds, and broth. Bring to a boil. Cover, reduce heat and simmer 10 minutes. Add noodles and cook another 3-5 minutes or noodles are done.
3. Stir in sour cream until blended and serve.

Nutrition Facts Per Serving

Calories 368 Total Carbs 12g Net Carbs 11g Protein 46g Fat 13g Sugar 5g Fiber 1g

Garlic Pork Chops

Prep time: 5 minutes, Cook time: 10 minutes, Serves: 6

Ingredients:

6 boneless pork loin chops, trim excess fat
What you'll need from store cupboard:
¼ cup lemon juice
2 drops liquid stevia
¼ cup low sodium soy sauce
¼ cup dry white wine
2 tbsps. garlic, diced fine
1 tbsp. vegetable oil
¼ tsp. black pepper

Instructions:

1. Combine lemon juice, liquid stevia, soy sauce, wine, garlic, and pepper in a 9x13 inch baking dish. Mix well.
2. Add pork chops, turning to coat. Cover and refrigerate at least 4 hours, or overnight, turning chops occasionally.
3. Heat oil in a large skillet over med-high heat. Add chops and cook 2-3 minutes per side.
4. Pour marinade over chops and bring to a boil. Reduce heat to low and simmer 2-3 minutes, or chops are desired doneness. Serve topped with sauce.

Nutrition Facts Per Serving

Calories 436 Total Carbs 14g Net Carbs 12g Protein 26g Fat 30g Sugar 12g Fiber 0g

Smoked Lamb & Apricot Kebabs

Prep time: 1 hour 10 minutes, Cook time: 15 minutes, Serves: 6

Ingredients:

2½ lbs. lamb stew meat
1 red onion, cut into chunks
½ cup plain yogurt
Juice of 1 lemon
What you'll need from store cupboard:
2 cups dried apricots
1½ tsps. smoked paprika
½ tsp. oregano
Black pepper, to taste
Boiling water

Instructions:

1. In a large bowl, whisk together yogurt, lemon juice, smoked paprika, oregano and pepper. Add the lamb and toss until well coated. Cover and refrigerate for at least 1 hour.
2. Place the apricots in a medium bowl. Cover with boiling water and let sit for at least 30 minutes.
3. Heat grill to med-high heat. Thread 6 skewers with piece of lamb, then apricot, then onion. Repeat.
4. Grill 2-3 minutes per side, until lambs is nicely browned on the outside. Serve.

Nutrition Facts Per Serving

Calories 401 Total Carbs 10g Net Carbs 8g Protein 55g Fat 14g Sugar 7g Fiber 2g

French Beef Onion Casserole

Prep time: 15 minutes, Cook time: 55 minutes, Serves: 8

Ingredients:

1 lb. lean ground beef
6 eggs
2 cups skim milk
1 cup Swiss cheese, grated
½ cup onion, diced
What you'll need from store cupboard:
10 oz. can condensed French onion soup
6 oz. pkg. herb stuffing mix
1 tbsp. Worcestershire sauce
1 tbsp. olive oil
1 tbsp. chili sauce
2 tsps. thyme
Nonstick cooking spray

Instructions:

1. Heat oven to 350 °F. Spray a 13x9-inch baking dish with cooking spray.
2. Heat oil in a large skillet over medium heat. Add beef and cook, breaking up with spatula, until no longer pink.Add onion, Worcestershire, and chili sauce, and cook 3-5 minutes, until onions are soft.
3. In a large bowl, beat eggs, soup, milk, ½ cup cheese, and 1 tsp. thyme. Add the dry stuffing mix and beef. Stir well, making sure to coat the stuffing mixture.
4. Transfer to prepared baking dish. Sprinkle with remaining cheese and thyme and let rest 15 minutes.
5. Bake 45 minutes or until a knife inserted in center comes out clean. Serve.

Nutrition Facts Per Serving

Calories 327 Total Carbs 23g Net Carbs 22g Protein 30g Fat 12g Sugar 7g Fiber 1g

Herbed Pork Tenderloin

Prep time: 5 minutes, Cook time: 4 hours, Serves: 4

Ingredients:

1 lb. pork tenderloin
What you'll need from store cupboard:
2 tsps. olive oil
1 tsp. sage
1 tsp. thyme
½ tsp. garlic, diced fine
Salt and pepper, to taste

Instructions:

1. Stir the oil and seasonings together in a small bowl.
2. Place tenderloin in the crock pot and pour seasoning mix over the top. Cover and cook on high 3-4 hours, or until pork reaches desired doneness. Serve.

Nutrition Facts Per Serving

Calories 183 Total Carbs 0g Net Carbs 0g Protein 30g Fat 6g Sugar 0g Fiber 0g

Asian Pork Meatball Soup, page 47

Cheddar Ham & Broccoli Soup, page 47

Beef Burgundy & Carrot Stew, page 47

Garlic Chicken & Cauliflower Rice Soup, page 48

Chapter 9 Soups and Stews Recipe

Asian Pork Meatball Soup

Prep time: 15 minutes, Cook time: 5 hours, Serves: 4

Ingredients:

½ lb. ground pork
4 cups mustard greens, torn
4 scallions, sliced thin
2 tsps. fresh ginger, peeled and grated fine
What you'll need from store cupboard:
4 cups low sodium chicken broth
2 tbsps. soy sauce
1 tbsp. vegetable oil
2 cloves garlic, diced fine
1 tsp. peppercorns, crushed
1 tsp. fish sauce
¾ tsp. red pepper flakes,
½ tsp. cumin seeds, chopped coarse
Sea salt and black pepper

Instructions:

1. In a large bowl, combine pork, garlic, ginger, and spices. Season with salt and pepper. Use your hands to combine all ingredients thoroughly.
2. Heat oil in a large skillet over medium heat. Form pork into 1-inch balls and cook in oil till brown on all sides. Use a slotted spoon to transfer the meatballs to a crock pot.
3. Add remaining ingredients and stir. Cover and cook on low 4-5 hours or until meatballs are cooked through. Serve.

Nutrition Facts Per Serving

Calories 156 Total Carbs 7g Net Carbs 5g Protein 19g Fat 6g Sugar 2g Fiber 2g

Beef Burgundy & Carrot Stew

Prep time: 15 minutes, Cook time: 8 hours, Serves: 4

Ingredients:

1 lb. sirloin steak, cut into bite size pieces
2 carrots, peeled and cut into 1-inch pieces
1 cup mushrooms, sliced
¾ cup pearl onions, thawed if frozen
What you'll need from store cupboard:
1 cup Burgundy wine
½ cup low sodium beef broth
3 cloves garlic, diced
2 tbsps. olive oil
1 bay leaf
1 tsp. marjoram
½ tsp. salt
½ tsp. thyme
¼ tsp. pepper

Instructions:

1. Heat the oil in a large skillet over med-high heat. Add steak and brown on all sides. Transfer to a crock pot.
2. Add remaining ingredients and stir to combine. Cover and cook on low 7-8 hours or until steak is tender and vegetables are cooked through. Discard the bay leaf before serving.

Nutrition Facts Per Serving

Calories 353 Total Carbs 8g Net Carbs 7g Protein 36g Fat 14g Sugar 3g Fiber 1g

Cheddar Ham & Broccoli Soup

Prep time: 10 minutes, Cook time: 6 hours, Serves: 8

Ingredients:

2 cups broccoli florets
2 cups cheddar cheese, grated
1½ cups ham, cut into small cubes
2 stalks celery, peeled and diced
1 onion, diced
What you'll need from store cupboard:
8 cups low sodium vegetable broth
2 tbsps. olive oil
1 bay leaf
¼ tsp. salt
⅛ tsp. black pepper

Instructions:

1. Heat the oil in a medium skillet over med-high heat. Add the onion and celery and cook, stirring frequently, about 5 minutes.
2. Add the broth, ham, celery mixture, and seasonings to a crock pot. Cover and cook on low 3-4 hours.
3. Add the broccoli and cook another 1-2 hours or until broccoli starts to get tender. Stir in cheese and cook until completely melted. Discard bay leaf and serve.

Nutrition Facts Per Serving

Calories 214 Total Carbs 8g Net Carbs 7g Protein 12g Fat 15g Sugar 2g Fiber 1g

Garlic Chicken & Cauliflower Rice Soup

Prep time: 20 minutes, Cook time: 5 hours, Serves: 6

Ingredients:

2 carrots, peeled and diced
2 stalks celery, peeled and diced
½ onion, diced
2 cups skim milk
2 cups cauliflower, riced
1 cup chicken, cooked and shredded
3 tbsps. nut butter

What you'll need from store cupboard:

4 cups low sodium chicken broth
5 cloves garlic, diced
½ tsp. rosemary
½ tsp. thyme
½ tsp. parsley
1 bay leaf

Instructions:

1. Melt nut butter in a large skillet over medium heat. Add carrots, celery, onion and garlic. Cook, stirring frequently, about 5 minutes. Place in crock pot.
2. Add chicken broth and seasonings. Cover and cook on low 4 hours.
3. Add in the chicken, milk and cauliflower rice. Cook another 60 minutes or until cauliflower is tender. Discard bay leaf before serving.

Nutrition Facts Per Serving

Calories 151 Total Carbs 10g Net Carbs 8g Protein 12g Fat 6g Sugar 6g Fiber 2g

Beef Zoodle and Tomato Stew

Prep time: 15 minutes, Cook time: 1 hour 25 minutes, Serves: 6

Ingredients:

1 lb. beef stew meat
4 large zucchinis, spiralize
3 celery stalks, diced
3 carrots, peeled and diced
½ red onion, diced

What you'll need from store cupboard:

14 oz. can tomatoes, diced
4 cups low-sodium beef broth
2 cloves garlic, diced fine
1-2 bay leaves
3 tbsps. Worcestershire sauce
2 tbsps. olive oil
1 tsp. thyme
½ tsp. cayenne pepper
¼ tsp. red pepper flakes
Salt and pepper, to taste
Freshly chopped parsley, to garnish

Instructions:

1. Heat oil in a large saucepan over medium heat. Add beef and cook until brown on all sides. Remove from pan and set aside.
2. Add the garlic to the pan and cook 30 seconds. Then stir in onion and red pepper flakes. Cook 1 minute and add the celery and carrots. Sweat the vegetables for 2 minutes, stirring occasionally.
3. Add the beef back to the pan with the Worcestershire, thyme, and cayenne pepper and stir. Season with salt and pepper to taste. Add the broth, tomatoes, and bay leaves and bring to a boil.
4. Reduce heat, cover and let simmer 40 minutes. Remove the cover and cook 35 minutes more or until stew thickens.
5. Divide the zucchini noodles evenly among four bowls. Ladle stew evenly over zucchini and let set for a few minutes to cook the zucchini. Top with fresh parsley and serve.

Nutrition Facts Per Serving

Calories 225 Total Carbs 13g Net Carbs 10g Protein 29g Fat 6g Sugar 8g Fiber 3g

Crab & Carrot Bisque

Prep time: 20 minutes, Cook time: 30 minutes, Serves: 8

Ingredients:

1 lb. lump crabmeat, cooked and shells removed
1 medium head cauliflower, separated into very small florets
1 white onion, diced fine
1 cup celery, diced fine
1 cup carrots, diced fine
1 cup nonfat half-n-half
1 tbsp. sherry
4 tbsps. nut butter

What you'll need from store cupboard:

6 cups chicken broth
1½ tsps. coarse salt
1 tsp. white pepper

Instructions:

1. In a large saucepan, over med-high heat, melt nut butter. Add celery, onion, and carrot. Cook, stirring frequently, until vegetables are tender.
2. Add in cauliflower, broth, salt, and pepper, and cook until soup starts to boil. Reduce heat to medium and cook 15 minutes, or until cauliflower is tender.
3. Pour into a blender and add cream and sherry. Process until combined and soup is smooth. Pour back into the saucepan.
4. Fold in crab and heat through. Serve.

Nutrition Facts Per Serving

Calories 201 Total Carbs 10g Net Carbs 7g Protein 14g Fat 11g Sugar 4g Fiber 3g

Beef & Onion Soup

Ingredients:
1½ lbs. beef stew meat
1 cup onion, diced
½ cup celery, diced
What you'll need from store cupboard:
6 cups water
½ cup lentils
2 cloves garlic, diced
2 bay leaves
2 tsps. salt
1 tsp. olive oil
Fresh ground black pepper

Instructions:
1. In a large skillet over med-high heat, heat oil. Add beef and brown on all sides. Use a slotted spoon to transfer the meat to a crock pot.
2. Add remaining ingredients, cover and cook on low 6-7 hours or until beef is tender. Discard bay leaves before serving.

Nutrition Facts Per Serving

Calories 213 Total Carbs 9g Net Carbs 5g Protein 29g Fat 6g Sugar 1g Fiber 4g

Beef Cauliflower Soup

Prep time: 15 minutes, Cook time: 7 hours, Serves: 6

Ingredients:
1 lb. lean ground beef, cooked and drained
2 stalks celery, sliced
1 large head of cauliflower, separated medium sized florets
1 tomato, diced
½ onion, diced
1 cup carrots, sliced thick
1 cup corn kernels
What you'll need from store cupboard:
4 cups water
1¾ cups low sodium beef broth
1½ cups tomato sauce
½ cup white cooking wine
1 tbsp. parsley

Instructions:
1. Place everything but the cauliflower in a crock pot. Cover and cook on low 5-6 hours or until vegetables are almost tender.
2. Add the cauliflower and cook another 60 minutes. Serve.

Nutrition Facts Per Serving

Calories 254 Total Carbs 20g Net Carbs 14g Protein 29g Fat 6g Sugar 9g Fiber 6g

Curried Chicken and Cauliflower Soup

Prep time: 15 minutes, Cook time: 20 minutes, Serves: 12

Ingredients:
2 carrots, diced
2 stalks celery, diced
1 onion, diced
3 cups chicken, cooked and cut in cubes
2 cups cauliflower, grated
1 cup nonfat half-n-half
¼ cup nut butter, cubed
What you'll need from store cupboard:
4½ cups low sodium vegetable broth
2 (12 oz.) can fat free evaporated milk
¾ cup + 2 tbsps. flour
1 tsp. salt
1 tsp. curry powder

Instructions:
1. Melt butter in a large pot over medium heat. Add carrots, celery, and onion and cook 2 minutes.
2. Stir in flour until well blended. Stir in seasonings. Slowly add milk and half-n-half. Bring to a boil, cook, stirring, 2 minutes or until thickened.
3. Slowly stir in broth. Add chicken and cauliflower and bring back to boil. Reduce heat and simmer 10 minutes, or until vegetable are tender. Serve.

Nutrition Facts Per Serving

Calories 204 Total Carbs 17g Net Carbs 15g Protein 17g Fat 7g Sugar 8g Fiber 1g

Cream Salmon Dill Soup

Prep time: 5 minutes, Cook time: 30 minutes, Serves: 4

Ingredients:
4 skinless salmon fillets, cut into pieces
1 green onion, diced fine
1 daikon radish, peeled and diced
½ cup heavy cream
2 tbsps. fresh dill, diced
2 tbsps. nut butter
What you'll need from store cupboard:
4 cups seafood stock or vegetable broth
½ cup white wine
Salt and black pepper

Instructions:
1. In a large saucepan, melt nut butter over med-high heat. Add onions and sauté for 1-2 minutes.
2. Add wine and cook until liquid is reduced by half.
3. Add the radish and broth. Cook until radish is tender, about 15 minutes. Add salmon, cream and dill and cook another 5-8 minutes until salmon is flaky. Salt and pepper to taste.

Nutrition Facts Per Serving

Calories 537 Total Carbs 8g Net Carbs 7g Protein 46g Fat 33g Sugar 2g Fiber 1g

Korean Radish Beef Soup

Prep time: 15 minutes, Cook time: 4 hours, Serves: 8

Ingredients:

1 pound beef, cut into cubes
1 Korean white radish, peeled and diced
1 cup green onions, diced
What you'll need from store cupboard:
1 gallon water
3 tbsps. soy sauce
1 tbsp. oil
1 tbsp. Sesame seeds, toasted
2 cloves garlic, diced fine
1 tsp. salt
1 tsp. pepper

Instructions:

1. Set crock pot to high and pour the water in to start heating.
2. In a small bowl, combine green onions, soy sauce, oil, sesame seeds, garlic, salt, and pepper. Divide evenly between two Ziploc bags.
3. Place the meat in one bag and the radish in the other. Let set for 1 hour.
4. Turn the crock pot down to low and add the contents of the meat bag. Let cook 1 hour, then add the contents of the radish bag. Cook another 3-4 hours.

Nutrition Facts Per Serving

Calories 120 Total Carbs 3g Net Carbs 2g Protein 18g Fat 4g Sugar 0g Fiber 1g

Mexican Beef and Tomato Stew

Prep time: 15 minutes, Cook time: 1 hours 30 minutes, Serves: 6

Ingredients:

1½ lbs. beef round steak, cut into ½-inch pieces
1¾ cups tomatoes, diced
1 cup carrots, sliced
1 cup onion, diced
¼ cup sweet red pepper, diced
1 jalapeno, seeded and diced
2 tbsps. cilantro, diced
What you'll need from store cupboard:
1¾ cups low sodium beef broth
1 clove garlic, diced
2 tbsps. flour
2 tbsps. water
1 tbsp. vegetable oil
1½ tsps. chili powder
½ tsp. salt

Instructions:

1. Heat the oil in a large pot over med-high heat. Add the steak and cook until brown on all sides.
2. Add the broth, carrots, onion, red pepper, jalapeno, garlic, and seasonings and bring to a low boil. Reduce heat to low, cover and simmer 45 minutes, stirring occasionally.
3. Add the tomatoes and continue cooking 15 minutes.
4. Stir the flour and water together in a measuring up until smooth. Add to stew with the cilantro and continue cooking another 20-30 minutes or until stew has thickened. Serve.

Nutrition Facts Per Serving

Calories 312 Total Carbs 9g Net Carbs 7g Protein 39g Fat 13g Sugar 4g Fiber 2g

Curried Mushroom & Cauliflower Soup

Prep time: 15 minutes, Cook time: 30 minutes, Serves: 4

Ingredients:

1 small (20 oz.) cauliflower, trimmed, chopped
5 cups mushrooms, sliced
1 leek, halved lengthways, thinly sliced
½ cup flat-leaf parsley, chopped
What you'll need from store cupboard:
4 cups low sodium chicken broth
4 tbsps. olive oil
3 tsps. curry powder
Nonstick cooking spray

Instructions:

1. Heat oven to 425 °F.
2. Spray two large baking sheets with cooking spray. Place cauliflower in one pan and mushrooms in the other. Drizzle each with 1½ tbsps. oil and sprinkle with 1½ tsps. curry powder.
3. Place cauliflower on the top rack of oven and mushrooms below, cook 20-25 minutes or until vegetables are tender.
4. In a large saucepan, heat remaining oil over medium heat. Add leek, cook 5 minutes, stirring occasionally, until soft. Add broth and bring to a boil. Add roasted vegetables and return to boil.
5. Remove from heat, use an immersion blender, and process until almost smooth. Stir in parsley and adjust seasonings to taste. Serve.

Nutrition Facts Per Serving

Calories 187 Total Carbs 11g Net Carbs 8g Protein 7g Fat 15g Sugar 4g Fiber 3g

Seafood Onion Chowder

Ingredients:

1½ lbs. frozen mixed seafood, thaw and cut into bite-sized pieces
3 celery stalks, diced
1½ cups onion, diced
½ cup nonfat half-n-half
4-5 tbsps. fresh dill, chopped

What you'll need from store cupboard:

2½ cups low sodium chicken broth
1½ cups white wine
1½ tbsps. olive oil
1½ tbsps. corn starch
1½ tbsps. cold water
1½ tsps. garlic, diced fine
Salt and pepper

Instructions:

1. Heat oil in a large soup pot over medium heat. Add onion and celery and cook until softened, about 5-7 minutes. Stir in garlic and cook for another 30 seconds.
2. Add wine to the pot and bring to a low boil, cooking until most of the liquid has disappeared.
3. Combine the corn starch and water in a small bowl and stir until dissolved. Add cornstarch mixture and chicken broth to the pan. Simmer for 7-10 minutes or until thickened, stirring occasionally.
4. Season the soup to taste with salt and pepper then add the seafood and dill to the pot. Simmer until seafood is cooked through, about 3-7 minutes. Stir in half-n-half and cook just until heated through. Serve garnished with more fresh dill if desired.

Nutrition Facts Per Serving

Calories 353 Total Carbs 16g Net Carbs 15g Protein 27g Fat 10g Sugar 3g Fiber 1g

Italian Vegetable Soup

Ingredients:

4 cups cabbage, chopped
2 celery stalks, diced
2 green bell peppers, diced
1 small onion, diced
2 cups fresh spinach, chopped
1 cup carrots, diced
1 cup green beans, cut in 1-inch pieces

What you'll need from store cupboard:

28 oz. can low sodium tomatoes, diced
6 cups low sodium vegetable broth
2 tbsps. tomato paste
1 tbsp. parsley
1 tbsp. basil
2 cloves garlic, diced fine
2 bay leaves
1½ tsps. Italian seasoning
Pepper to taste

Instructions:

1. Place all the vegetables in a large crock pot.
2. Add canned tomatoes, broth, tomato paste, bay leaves, Italian seasoning, and pepper and stir to combine.
3. Cover and cook on high for 5 hours. Add parsley, basil and spinach and cook for 5 minutes more.

Nutrition Facts Per Serving

Calories 85 Total Carbs 20g Net Carbs 15g Protein 3g Fat 1g Sugar 10g Fiber 5g

BBQ Grilled Tofu & Veggie Skewers，page 53

Curry Tofu，page 53

Orange Tofu with Broccoli，page 53

Mayo Tofu Salad Sandwiches，page 54

Chapter 10 Meatless Main Dishes Recipe

BBQ Grilled Tofu & Veggie Skewers

Prep time: 15 minutes, Cook time: 15 minutes, Serves: 6

Ingredients:

1 block tofu
2 small zucchinis, sliced
1 red bell pepper, cut into 1-inch cubes
1 yellow bell pepper, cut into 1-inch cubes
1 red onion, cut into 1-inch cubes
2 cups cherry tomatoes

What you'll need from store cupboard:

2 tbsps. lite soy sauce
3 tsps. Basic BBQ sauce (chapter 13)
2 tsps. sesame seeds
Salt & pepper, to taste
Nonstick cooking spray

Instructions:

1. Press tofu to extract liquid, for about half an hour. Then, cut tofu into cubes and marinate in soy sauce for at least 15 minutes.
2. Heat the grill to med-high heat. Spray the grill rack with cooking spray.
3. Assemble skewers with tofu alternating with vegetables.
4. Grill 2-3 minutes per side until vegetables start to soften, and tofu is golden brown. At the very end of cooking time, season with salt and pepper and brush with barbecue sauce. Serve garnished with sesame seeds.

Nutrition Facts Per Serving

Calories 64 Total Carbs 10g Net Carbs 7g Protein 5g Fat 2g Sugar 6g Fiber 3g

Orange Tofu with Broccoli

Prep time: 15 minutes, Cook time: 2 hours, Serves: 4

Ingredients:

1 package extra firm tofu, pressed for at least 15 minutes, cut into cubes
2 cups broccoli florets, fresh
1 tbsp. nut butter

What you'll need from store cupboard:

¼ cup orange juice
¼ cup reduced sodium soy sauce
2 drops liquid stevia
2 cloves garlic, diced fine

Instructions:

1. Melt nut butter in a medium skillet, over medium high heat. Add tofu and garlic and cook, stirring occasionally until tofu starts to brown, about 5-10 minutes. Transfer to crock pot.
2. Whisk the wet ingredients together in a small bowl. Pour over tofu and add the broccoli.
3. Cover and cook on high 90 minutes, or on low 2 hours.
4. Serve over cauliflower rice (chapter 4).

Nutrition Facts Per Serving

Calories 137 Total Carbs 24g Net Carbs 22g Protein 4g Fat 4g Sugar 20g Fiber 2g

Curry Tofu

Prep time: 10 minutes, Cook time: 2 hours, Serves: 4

Ingredients:

2 cups green bell pepper, diced
1 cup firm tofu, cut into cubes
1 onion, peeled and diced

What you'll need from store cupboard:

1½ cups canned coconut milk
1 cup tomato paste
2 cloves garlic, diced fine
2 tbsps. raw peanut butter
1 tbsp. garam masala
1 tbsp. curry powder
1½ tsps. salt

Instructions:

1. Add all ingredients, except the tofu to a blender or food processor. Process until thoroughly combined.
2. Pour into a crock pot and add the tofu. Cover and cook on high 2 hours.
3. Stir well and serve over cauliflower rice.

Nutrition Facts Per Serving

Calories 389 Total Carbs 28g Net Carbs 20g Protein 13g Fat 28g Sugar 16g Fiber 8g

Mayo Tofu Salad Sandwiches

Prep time: 15 minutes, Total time: 20 minutes, Serves: 4

Ingredients:

1 pkg. silken firm tofu, pressed
4 lettuce leaves
2 green onions, diced
¼ cup celery, diced
What you'll need from store cupboard:
8 slices bread
¼ cup lite mayonnaise
2 tbsps. sweet pickle relish
1 tbsp. Dijon mustard
¼ tsp. turmeric
¼ tsp. salt
⅛ tsp. cayenne pepper

Instructions:

1. Press tofu between layers of paper towels for 15 minutes to remove excess moisture. Cut into small cubes.
2. In a medium bowl, stir together remaining ingredients. Fold in tofu. Spread over 4 slices of bread. Top with a lettuce leaf and another slice of bread. Serve.

Nutrition Facts Per Serving

Calories 378 Total Carbs 15g Net Carbs 13g Protein 24g Fat 20g Sugar 2g Fiber 2g

Garlic Tempeh Lettuce Wraps

Prep time: 5 minutes, Cook time: 5 minutes, Serves: 2

Ingredients:

1 pkg. tempeh, crumbled
1 head butter-leaf lettuce
½ red bell pepper, diced
½ onion, diced
What you'll need from store cupboard:
1 tbsp. garlic, diced fine
1 tbsp. olive oil
1 tbsp. low-sodium soy sauce
1 tsp. ginger,
1 tsp. onion powder
1 tsp. garlic powder

Instructions:

1. Heat oil and garlic in a large skillet over medium heat.
2. Add onion, tempeh, and bell pepper and sauté for 3 minutes.
3. Add soy sauce and spices and cook for another 2 minutes.
4. Spoon mixture into lettuce leaves.

Nutrition Facts Per Serving

Calories 130 Total Carbs 14g Net Carbs 10g Protein 8g Fat 5g Sugar 2g Fiber 4g

Crock Pot Chili Stroganoff

Prep time: 10 minutes, Cook time: 2 hours, Serves: 2

Ingredients:

8 cups mushrooms, cut into quarters
1 onion, halved and sliced thin
4 tbsps. fresh parsley, chopped
1½ tbsps. low fat sour cream
What you'll need from store cupboard:
1 cup low sodium vegetable broth
3 cloves garlic, diced fine
2 tsps. smoked paprika
Salt and pepper to taste

Instructions:

1. Add all ingredients, except sour cream and parsley to crock pot.cover and cook on high 2 hours.
2. Stir in sour cream and serve garnished with parsley.

Nutrition Facts Per Serving

Calories 111 Total Carbs 18g Net Carbs 14g Protein 10g Fat 2g Sugar 8g Fiber 4g

Tofu & Cauliflower Bento

Prep time: 15 minutes, Cook time: 10 minutes, Serves: 4

Ingredients:

1 pkg. extra firm tofu
1 red bell pepper, sliced
1 orange bell pepper, sliced
2 cups cauliflower rice, cooked
2 cups broccoli, chopped
¼ cup green onion, sliced
What you'll need from store cupboard:
2 tbsps. low-sodium soy sauce
1 tbsp. olive oil
1 tsp. ginger,
1 tsp. garlic powder
1 tsp. onion powder
1 tsp. chili paste

Instructions:

1. Remove tofu from package and press with paper towels to absorb all excess moisture, let set for 15 minutes.
2. Chop tofu into cubes. Add tofu and seasonings to a large Ziploc bag and shake to coat.
3. Heat oil in a large skillet over medium heat. Add tofu and vegetables and cook, stirring frequently, 5-8 minutes, until tofu is browned on all sides and vegetables are tender.
4. To serve, place ½ cup cauliflower rice on 4 plates and top evenly with tofu mixture.

Nutrition Facts Per Serving

Calories 93 Total Carbs 12g Net Carbs 8g Protein 7g Fat 3g Sugar 5g Fiber 4g

Authentic Pad Thai

Prep time: 15 minutes, Cook time: 30 minutes, Serves: 6

Ingredients:

12 oz. extra firm tofu organic, cut into 1-inch cubes
2 zucchinis, shredded into long zoodles
1 carrot, grated
3 cups bean sprouts
2 Green onions sliced
1 cup red cabbage, shredded
¼ cup cilantro, chopped
What you'll need from store cupboard:
¼ cup lime juice
2 cloves garlic, diced fine
2 tbsps. reduced fat peanut butter
2 tbsps. tamari
1 tbsp. sesame seeds
½ tbsp. sesame oil
2 tsps. red chili flakes

Instructions:

1. Heat half the oil in a saucepan over medium heat. Add tofu and cook until it starts to brown, about 5 minutes. Add garlic and stir until light brown.
2. Add zucchini, carrot, cabbage, lime juice, peanut butter, tamari, and chili flakes. Stir to combine all ingredients. Cook, stirring frequently, until vegetables are tender, about 5 minutes. Add bean sprouts and remove from heat.
3. Serve topped with green onions, sesame seeds and cilantro.

Nutrition Facts Per Serving

Calories 134 Total Carbs 13g Net Carbs 11g Protein 12g Fat 6g Sugar 3g Fiber 2g

Mexican Scrambled Eggs & Veggie

Prep time: 15 minutes, Cook time: 5 minutes, Serves: 4

Ingredients:

8 egg whites
4 egg yolks
3 tomatoes, cut in ½-inch pieces
1 jalapeno pepper, slice thin
½ avocado, cut in ½-inch pieces
½ red onion, diced fine
½ head Romaine lettuce, torn
½ cup cilantro, chopped
2 tbsps. fresh lime juice
What you'll need from store cupboard:
12 tortilla chips, broken into small pieces
2 tbsps. water
1 tbsp. olive oil
¾ tsp. pepper, divided
½ tsp. salt, divided

Instructions:

1. In a medium bowl, combine tomatoes, avocado, onion, jalapeno, cilantro, lime juice, ¼ tsp. salt, and ¼ tsp. pepper.
2. In a large bowl, whisk egg whites, egg yolks, water, and remaining salt and pepper. Stir in tortilla chips.
3. Heat oil in a large skillet over medium heat. Add egg mixture and cook, stirring frequently, 3-5 minutes, or desired doneness.
4. To serve, divide lettuce leaves among 4 plates. Add scrambled egg mixture and top with salsa.

Nutrition Facts Per Serving

Calories 280 Total Carbs 10g Net Carbs 6g Protein 15g Fat 21g Sugar 4g Fiber 4g

Healthy Teriyaki Tofu Burger

Prep time: 15 minutes, Cook time: 15 minutes, Serves: 2

Ingredients:

2 (3 oz.) tofu portions, extra firm, pressed between paper towels 15 minutes
¼ red onion, sliced
2 tbsps. carrot, grated
1 tsp. nut butter
Butter leaf lettuce
What you'll need from store cupboard:
2 100% whole wheat sandwich thins
1 tbsp. teriyaki marinade
1 tbsp. Sriracha
1 tsp. red chili flakes

Instructions:

1. Heat grill, or charcoal, to a medium heat.
2. Marinate tofu in teriyaki marinade, red chili flakes and Sriracha.
3. Melt nut butter in a small skillet over med-high heat. Add onions and cook until caramelized, about 5 minutes.
4. Grill tofu for 3-4 minutes per side.
5. To assemble, place tofu on bottom roll. Top with lettuce, carrot, and onion. Add top of the roll and serve.

Nutrition Facts Per Serving

Calories 178 Total Carbs 27g Net Carbs 20g Protein 12g Fat 5g Sugar 5g Fiber 7g

Cinnamon Candied Pecans，page 57

Hot Buffalo Bites，page 57

Banana Oat Nut Cookies，page 57

Chinese Chicken Wings，page 57

Chapter 11 Snacks Recipe

Cinnamon Candied Pecans

Prep time: 5 minutes, Cook time: 10 minutes, Serves: 6

Ingredients:

1½ tsps. nut butter
What you'll need from store cupboard:
1½ cups pecan halves
2½ tbsps. Splenda, divided
1 tsp. cinnamon
¼ tsp. ginger
⅛ tsp. cardamom
⅛ tsp. salt

Instructions:

1. In a small bowl, stir together 1½ tsps. Splenda, cinnamon, ginger, cardamom and salt. Set aside.
2. Melt butter in a medium skillet over med-low heat. Add pecans, and two tbsps. Splenda. Reduce heat to low and cook, stirring occasionally, until sweetener melts, about 5 to 8 minutes.
3. Add spice mixture to the skillet and stir to coat pecans. Spread mixture to parchment paper and let cool for 10-15 minutes. Store in an airtight container. Serving size is ¼ cup.

Nutrition Facts Per Serving

Calories 173 Total Carbs 8g Net Carbs 6g Protein 2g Fat 16g Sugar 6g Fiber 2g

Banana Oat Nut Cookies

Prep time: 10 minutes, Cook time: 15 minutes, Serves: 18

Ingredients:

1½ cups banana, mashed
What you'll need from store cupboard:
2 cups oats
1 cup raisins
1 cup walnuts
⅓ cup sunflower oil
1 tsp. vanilla
½ tsp. salt

Instructions:

1. Heat oven to 350 °F.
2. In a large bowl, combine oats, raisins, walnuts, and salt.
3. In a medium bowl, mix banana, oil, and vanilla. Stir into oat mixture until combined. Let rest 15 minutes.
4. Drop by rounded tablespoonful onto 2 ungreased cookie sheets. Bake 15 minutes, or until a light golden brown. Cool and store in an airtight container. Serving size is 2 cookies.

Nutrition Facts Per Serving

Calories 148 Total Carbs 16g Net Carbs 14g Protein 3g Fat 9g Sugar 6g Fiber 2g

Hot Buffalo Bites

Prep time: 5 minutes, Cook time: 10 minutes, Serves: 4

Ingredients:

1 egg
½ head of cauliflower, separated into florets
What you'll need from store cupboard:
1 cup panko bread crumbs
1 cup low-fat ranch dressing
½ cup hot sauce
½ tsp. salt
½ tsp. garlic powder
Black pepper
Nonstick cooking spray

Instructions:

1. Heat oven to 400 °F. Spray a baking sheet with cooking spray.
2. Place the egg in a medium bowl and mix in the salt, pepper and garlic. Place the panko crumbs into a small bowl.
3. Dip the florets first in the egg then into the panko crumbs. Place in a single layer on prepared pan.
4. Bake 8-10 minutes, stirring halfway through, until cauliflower is golden brown and crisp on the outside.
5. In a small bowl stir the dressing and hot sauce together. Use for dipping.

Nutrition Facts Per Serving

Calories 132 Total Carbs 15g Net Carbs 14g Protein 6g Fat 5g Sugar 4g Fiber 1g

Chinese Chicken Wings

Prep time: 5 minutes, Cook time: 30 minutes, Serves: 3

Ingredients:

24 chicken wings
What you'll need from store cupboard:
6 tbsps. soy sauce
6 tbsps. Chinese 5 spice
Salt & pepper
Nonstick cooking spray

Instructions:

1. Heat oven to 350 °F. Spray a baking sheet with cooking spray.
2. Combine the soy sauce, 5 spice, salt, and pepper in a large bowl. Add the wings and toss to coat.
3. Pour the wings onto the prepared pan. Bake 15 minutes. Turn chicken over and cook another 15 minutes until chicken is cooked through.
4. Serve with your favorite low carb dipping sauce (see chapter 13).

Nutrition Facts Per Serving

Calories 178 Total Carbs 8g Net Carbs 6g Protein 12g Fat 11g Sugar 1g Fiber 0g

Almond Cheese Bites

Prep time: 5 minutes, Chill time: 30 minutes, Serves: 6

Ingredients:

½ cup reduced-fat cream cheese, soft
What you'll need from store cupboard:
½ cup almonds, ground fine
¼ cup almond butter
2 drops liquid stevia

Instructions:

1. In a large bowl, beat cream cheese, almond butter and stevia on high speed until mixture is smooth and creamy. Cover and chill 30 minutes.
2. Use your hands to shape the mixture into 12 balls.
3. Place the ground almonds in a shallow plate. Roll the balls in the nuts completely covering all sides. Store in an airtight container in the refrigerator.

Nutrition Facts Per Serving

Calories 68 Total Carbs 3g Net Carbs 2 Protein 5g Fat 5g Sugar 0g Fiber 1g

Lemon Cauliflower Puree

Prep time: 5 minutes, Cook time: 15 minutes, serves 6

Ingredients:

3 cups cauliflower florets
3 tbsps. fresh lemon juice
What you'll need from store cupboard:
5 cloves garlic, divided
5 tbsps. olive oil, divided
2 tbsps. water
1½ tbsps. Tahini paste
1¼ tsps. salt, divided
Smoked paprika and extra olive oil for serving

Instructions:

1. In a microwave safe bowl, combine cauliflower, water, 2 tbsps. oil, ½ tsp. salt, and 3 whole cloves garlic. Microwave on high 15 minutes, or until cauliflower is soft and darkened.
2. Transfer mixture to a food processor or blender and process until almost smooth. Add tahini paste, lemon juice, remaining garlic cloves, remaining oil, and salt. Blend until almost smooth.
3. Place the hummus in a bowl and drizzle lightly with olive oil and a sprinkle or two of paprika. Serve with your favorite raw vegetables.

Nutrition Facts Per Serving

Calories 107 Total Carbs 5g Net Carbs 3g Protein 2g Fat 10g Sugar 1g Fiber 2g

Garlic Pita Crisps

Prep time: 5 minutes, Cook time: 15 minutes, Serves: 8

Ingredients:

½ cup mozzarella cheese
¼ cup nut butter, melted
What you'll need from store cupboard:
4 whole-wheat pita pocket halves
3 tbsps. reduced fat parmesan
½ tsp. garlic powder
½ tsp. onion powder
¼ tsp. salt
¼ tsp. pepper
Nonstick cooking spray

Instructions:

1. Heat oven to 400 °F. Spray a baking sheet with cooking spray.
2. Cut each pita pocket in half. Cut each half into 2 triangles. Place, rough side up, on prepared pan.
3. In a small bowl, whisk together nut butter, parmesan and seasonings. Spread each triangle with nut butter mixture. Sprinkle mozzarella over top.
4. Bake 12-15 minutes or until golden brown.

Nutrition Facts Per Serving

Calories 131 Total Carbs 14g Net Carbs 12g Protein 4g Fat 7g Sugar 1g Fiber 2g

Chili Tortilla Chips

Prep time: 5 minutes, Cook time: 15 minutes, Serves: 10

Ingredients:

12 6-inch corn tortillas, cut into 8 triangles
3 tbsps. lime juice
What you'll need from store cupboard:
1 tsp. cumin
1 tsp. chili powder

Instructions:

1. Heat oven to 350 °F.
2. Place tortilla triangles in a single layer on a large baking sheet.
3. In a small bowl stir together spices.
4. Sprinkle half the lime juice over tortillas, followed by ½ the spice mixture. Bake 7 minutes.
5. Remove from oven and turn tortillas over. Sprinkle with remaining lime juice and spices. Bake another 8 minutes or until crisp, but not brown. Serve with your favorite salsa, serving size is 10 chips.

Nutrition Facts Per Serving

Calories 65 Total Carbs 14g Net Carbs 12g Protein 2g Fat 1g Sugar 0g Fiber 2g

Cinnamon Apple Popcorn with Walnuts

Prep time: 30 minutes, Cook time: 50 minutes, Serves: 11

Ingredients:

4 tbsps. nut butter, melted
What you'll need from store cupboard:
10 cups plain popcorn
2 cups dried apple rings, unsweetened and chopped
½ cup walnuts, chopped
2 tbsps. Splenda
1 tsp. cinnamon
½ tsp. vanilla

Instructions:

1. Heat oven to 250 °F.
2. Place chopped apples in a 9x13-inch baking dish and bake 20 minutes. Remove from oven and stir in popcorn and nuts.
3. In a small bowl, whisk together nut butter, vanilla, Splenda, and cinnamon. Drizzle evenly over popcorn and toss to coat.
4. Bake 30 minutes, stirring quickly every 10 minutes. If apples start to turn a dark brown, remove immediately.
5. Pout onto waxed paper to cool at least 30 minutes. Store in an airtight container. Serving size is 1 cup.

Nutrition Facts Per Serving

Calories 133 Total Carbs 14g Net Carbs 11g Protein 3g Fat 8g Sugar 7g Fiber 3g

Spicy Mixed Nuts

Prep time: 5 minutes, Cook time: 10 minutes, Serves: 6

Ingredients:

½ cup whole almonds
½ cup pecan halves
½ cup walnut halves
What you'll need from store cupboard:
1 tsp. sunflower oil
½ tsp. cumin
½ tsp. curry powder
⅛ tsp. cayenne pepper
Dash of white pepper

Instructions:

1. Heat oven to 350 °F.
2. Place the nuts in a large bowl. Add the oil and toss to coat.
3. Stir the spices together in a small bowl. Add to nuts and toss to coat.
4. Spread nuts on a large baking sheet in a single layer. Bake 10 minutes.
5. Remove from oven and let cool. Store in airtight container. Serving size is ¼ cup.

Nutrition Facts Per Serving

Calories 257 Total Carbs 5g Net Carbs 1g Protein 6g Fat 25g Sugar 1g Fiber 4g

Cranberry and Almond Granola Bars

Prep time: 15 minutes, Cook time: 20 minutes, Serves: 12

Ingredients:

1 egg
1 egg white
What you'll need from store cupboard:
2 cups low-fat granola
¼ cup dried cranberries, sweetened
¼ cup almonds, chopped
2 tbsps. Splenda
1 tsp. almond extract
½ tsp. cinnamon

Instructions:

1. Heat oven to 350 °F. Line the bottom and sides of an 8-inch baking dish with parchment paper.
2. In a large bowl, combine dry ingredients including the cranberries.
3. In a small bowl, whisk together egg, egg white and extract. Pour over dry ingredients and mix until combined.
4. Press mixture into the prepared pan. Bake 20 minutes or until light brown.
5. Cool in the pan for 5 minutes. Then carefully lift the bars from the pan onto a cutting board. Use a sharp knife to cut into 12 bars. Cool completely and store in an airtight container.

Nutrition Facts Per Serving

Calories 85 Total Carbs 14g Net Carbs 13g Protein 3g Fat 3g Sugar 5g Fiber 1g

Zucchini Fries

Prep time: 10 minutes, Cook time: 10 minutes, Serves: 4

Ingredients:

3 zucchinis, slice ¼ - ⅛-inch thick
2 eggs
What you'll need from store cupboard:
½ cup sunflower oil
⅓ cup coconut flour
¼ cup reduced fat Parmesan cheese
1 tbsp. water

Instructions:

1. Heat oil in a large skillet over medium heat.
2. In a shallow bowl whisk the egg and water together.
3. In another shallow bowl, stir flour and parmesan together.
4. Coat zucchini in the egg then flour mixture. Add, in a single layer, to the skillet. Cook 2 minutes per side until golden brown. Transfer to paper towel lined plate. Repeat.
5. Serve immediately with your favorite dipping sauce.

Nutrition Facts Per Serving

Calories 138 Total Carbs 6g Net Carbs 4g Protein 6g Fat 11g Sugar 3g Fiber 2g

Crispy Apple Fries

Prep time: 15 minutes, Cook time: 10 minutes, Serves: 8

Ingredients:

3 apples, peeled, cored, and sliced into ½-inch pieces
¼ cup reduced fat nut butter, melted
2 tbsps. walnuts, chopped

What you'll need from store cupboard:

¼ cup quick oats
3 tbsps. light brown sugar
2 tbsps. whole wheat flour
1 tsp. cinnamon
⅛ tsp. salt

Instructions:

1. Heat oven to 425 °F. Put a wire rack on a large cookie sheet.
2. Add oats and walnuts to a food processor or blender and process until the mixture resembles flour.
3. Place the oat mixture in a shallow pan and add brown sugar, flour, cinnamon, and salt, mix well. Pour melted butter in a separate shallow pan.
4. Dip apple slices in nut butter, then roll in oat mixture to coat completely. Place on wire rack.
5. Bake 10-12 minutes or until golden brown. Let cool before serving.

Nutrition Facts Per Serving

Calories 146 Total Carbs 20g Net Carbs 17g Protein 1g Fat 7g Sugar 13g Fiber 3g

Parmesan Sticks

Prep time: 1 hour 10 minutes, Cook time: 30 minutes, Serves: 4

Ingredients:

8 string cheese sticks, halved
2 eggs, beaten

What you'll need from store cupboard:

1 cup reduced fat parmesan cheese
½ cup sunflower oil
1 tbsp. Italian seasoning
1 clove garlic, diced fine
Homemade Marinara Sauce, (chapter 13)

Instructions:

1. Heat oil in a pot over med-high heat.
2. In a medium bowl, combine parmesan cheese, Italian seasoning and garlic.
3. In a small bowl, beat the eggs.
4. Dip string cheese in eggs then in parmesan mixture to coat, pressing coating into cheese.
5. Place in hot oil and cook until golden brown. Transfer to paper towel lined plate. Serve warm with Homemade Marinara Sauce.

Nutrition Facts Per Serving

Calories 290 Total Carbs 3g Net Carbs 2g Protein 24g Fat 20g Sugar 0g Fiber 0g

Soft Lemon Bars

Prep time: 15 minutes, Chill time: 2 hours, Serves: 20

Ingredients:

8 oz. low fat cream cheese, soft
⅓ cup nut butter, melted
3 tbsps. fresh lemon juice

What you'll need from store cupboard:

12 oz. evaporated milk
1 pkg. lemon gelatin, sugar free
1½ cups graham cracker crumbs
1 cup boiling water
¾ cup Splenda
1 tsp. vanilla

Instructions:

1. Pour milk into a large, metal bowl, place beaters in the bowl, cover and chill 2 hours.
2. In a small bowl, combine cracker crumbs and butter, reserve 1 tablespoon. Press the remaining mixture on the bottom of a 13x9-inch baking dish. Cover and chill until set.
3. In a small bowl, dissolve gelatin in boiling water. Stir in lemon juice and let cool.
4. In a large bowl, beat cream cheese, Splenda and vanilla until smooth. Add gelatin and mix well.
5. Beat the chilled milk until soft peaks form. Fold into cream cheese mixture. Pour over chilled crust and sprinkle with reserved crumbs. Cover and chill 2 hours before serving.

Nutrition Facts Per Serving

Calories 126 Total Carbs 15g Net Carbs 14g Protein 3g Fat 5g Sugar 10g Fiber 0g

Nutmeg Apple Chips

Prep time: 5 minutes, Cook time: 10 minutes, Serves: 2

Ingredients:

1 medium apple, sliced thin

What you'll need from store cupboard:

¼ tsp. cinnamon
¼ tsp. nutmeg
Nonstick cooking spray

Instructions:

1. Heat oven to 375 °F. Spray a baking sheet with cooking spray.
2. Place apples in a mixing bowl and add spices. Toss to coat.
3. Arrange apples, in a single layer, on prepared pan. Bake 4 minutes, turn apples over and bake 4 minutes more.
4. Serve immediately or store in airtight container.

Nutrition Facts Per Serving

Calories 58 Total Carbs 15g Net Carbs 12g Protein 0g Fat 0g Sugar 11g Fiber 3g

Cinnamon Roasted Pumpkin Seeds

Prep time: 10 minutes, Cook time: 30 minutes, Serves: 8

Ingredients:
2 cups raw fresh pumpkin seeds, wash and pat dry
1 tbsp. nut butter
What you'll need from store cupboard:
1 tsp. liquid stevia
1 tbsp. coconut oil
1 tsp. cinnamon

Instructions:
1. Heat oven to 275 °F. Line a baking sheet with parchment paper, making sure it hangs over both ends.
2. Place the pumpkin seeds in a medium bowl.
3. In a small microwave safe bowl, add butter, coconut oil, and liquid stevia. Microwave until the butter melts. Pour the butter mixture over the pumpkin seeds and stir. Add the cinnamon and stir again.
4. Dump the pumpkin seeds into the middle of the paper and place it in the oven. Bake for 30-40 minutes until the seeds are a deep golden brown, stirring every 10 minutes.
5. When the seeds are roasted, remove from the oven and stir again. Stir a few times as they cool to keep them from sticking in one big lump. Enjoy the seeds once they are cool enough to eat. Store uncovered for up to one week. Serving size is ¼ cup.

Nutrition Facts Per Serving

Calories 267 Total Carbs 13g Net Carbs 12g Protein 8g Fat 22g Sugar 7g Fiber 1g

Peanut Butter Oatmeal Bars

Prep time: 5 minutes, Cook time: 10 minutes, Serves: 10

Ingredients:
½ cup almond milk, unsweetened
What you'll need from store cupboard:
1 cup oats
2 drops liquid stevia
6 tbsps. raw peanut butter
2 tbsps. peanuts, chopped
1 tsp. pure vanilla

Instructions:
1. Heat oven to 325 °F. Line a cookie sheet with parchment paper.
2. Place all ingredients, except the peanuts, into a food processor. Process until you have a sticky dough. Use your hands to mix in the peanuts.
3. Separate the dough into 10 equal balls on the prepared cookie sheet. Shape into squares or bars. Press the bars flat to ¼-inch thickness.
4. Bake 8-12 minutes, or until the tops are nicely browned. Remove from oven and cool completely. The bars will be soft at first but will stiffen as they cool.

Nutrition Facts Per Serving

Calories 125 Total Carbs 14g Net Carbs 12g Protein 4g Fat 6g Sugar 1g Fiber 2g

Garlic Onion Rings

Prep time: 5 minutes, Cook time: 15 minutes, Serves: 4

Ingredients:
1 large onion, slice ½-inch thick
1 egg
What you'll need from store cupboard:
¼ cup sunflower oil
2 tbsps. coconut flour
2 tbsps. reduced fat parmesan cheese
¼ tsp. parsley flakes
⅛ tsp. garlic powder
⅛ tsp. cayenne pepper
Salt to taste

Instructions:
1. Heat oil in a large skillet over med-high heat.
2. In a shallow bowl, combine flour, parmesan, and seasonings.
3. Beat the egg.
4. Separate onion slices into individual rings and place in large bowl, add beaten egg and toss to coat well. Let rest 1-2 minutes.
5. In small batches, coat onion in flour mixture and add to skillet. Cook 1-2 minutes per side, or until golden brown. Transfer to paper towel lined cookie sheet.
6. Serve with Sugar Free Ketchup, (chapter 13), or your favorite dipping sauce.

Nutrition Facts Per Serving

Calories 184 Total Carbs 8g Net Carbs 5g Protein 3g Fat 16g Sugar 2g Fiber 3g

Apple Oat Crisp, **page 63**

Lemon Blackberry Crostata, **page 63**

Baked Custard with Maple Syrup, **page 63**

Lemon Blueberry Cupcakes, **page 64**

Chapter 12 Desserts Recipe

Apple Oat Crisp

Prep time: 20 minutes, Cook time: 30 minutes, Serves: 8

Ingredients:

5 cups Granny Smith apples, peeled and sliced
3 tbsps. nut butter
What you'll need from store cupboard:
½ cup rolled oats
¼ cup + 2 tbsps. Splenda
3 tbsps. flour
1 tsp. lemon juice
¾ tsp. apple pie spice, divided

Instructions:

1. Heat oven to 375 °F.
2. In a large bowl, combine apples, 2 tbsps. Splenda, lemon juice, and ½ tsp. apple pie spice. Mix to thoroughly coat apples.
3. Place apples in a 2-quart square baking pan.
4. In a medium bowl, combine oats, flour, ¼ cup Splenda, and remaining apple pie spice. With a pastry knife, cut in nut butter until mixture resembles coarse crumbs. Sprinkle evenly over apples.
5. Bake 30-35 minutes, or until apples are tender and topping is golden brown. Serve warm.

Nutrition Facts Per Serving

Calories 153 Total Carbs 27g Net Carbs 23g Protein 1g Fat 5g Sugar 18g Fiber 4g

Baked Custard with Maple Syrup

Prep time: 5 minutes, Cook time: 1 hour 15 minutes, Serves: 6

Ingredients:

2½ cups nonfat half-and-half
½ cup egg substitute
What you'll need from store cupboard:
3 cups boiling water
¼ cup Splenda
2 tbsps. sugar free maple syrup
2 tsps. vanilla
Dash nutmeg
Nonstick cooking spray

Instructions:

1. Heat oven to 325 °F. Lightly spray 6 custard cups or ramekins with cooking spray.
2. In a large bowl, whisk together half-n-half, egg substitute, Splenda, vanilla, and nutmeg. Pour evenly into prepared custard cups. Place cups in a 13x9-inch baking dish.
3. Pour boiling water around, being careful not to splash it into, the cups. Bake 1 hour 15 minutes, centers will not be completely set.
4. Remove cups from pan and cool completely. Cover and chill overnight.
5. Just before serving, drizzle with the maple syrup.

Nutrition Facts Per Serving

Calories 190 Total Carbs 15g Net Carbs 11g Protein 5g Fat 12g Sugar 8g Fiber 0g

Lemon Blackberry Crostata

Prep time: 10 minutes, Cook time: 20 minutes, Serves: 6

Ingredients:

1 9-inch pie crust, unbaked
2 cups fresh blackberries
Juice and zest of 1 lemon
2 tbsps. nut butter, soft
What you'll need from store cupboard:
3 tbsps. Splenda, divided
2 tbsps. cornstarch

Instructions:

1. Heat oven to 425 °F. Line a large baking sheet with parchment paper and unroll pie crust in pan.
2. In a medium bowl, combine blackberries, 2 tbsps. Splenda, lemon juice and zest, and cornstarch. Spoon onto crust leaving a 2-inch edge. Fold and crimp the edges.
3. Dot the berries with 1 tbsp. butter. Brush the crust edge with remaining butter and sprinkle crust and fruit with remaining Splenda.
4. Bake 20-22 minutes or until golden brown. Cool before cutting and serving.

Nutrition Facts Per Serving

Calories 206 Total Carbs 24g Net Carbs 21g Protein 2g Fat 11g Sugar 9g Fiber 3g

Lemon Blueberry Cupcakes

Prep time: 5 minutes, Cook time: 10 minutes, Serves: 5

Ingredients:

4 eggs
½ cup coconut milk
½ cup blueberries
2 tbsps. lemon zest
What you'll need from store cupboard:
½ cup + 1 tsp. coconut flour
¼ cup Splenda
¼ cup coconut oil, melted
1 tsp. baking soda
½ tsp. lemon extract
¼ tsp. stevia extract
Pinch salt

Instructions:

1. In a small bowl, toss berries in the 1 tsp. of flour.
2. In a large bowl, stir together remaining flour, Splenda, baking soda, salt, and zest.
3. Add the remaining ingredients and mix well. Fold in the blueberries.
4. Divide batter evenly into 5 coffee cups. Microwave, one at a time, for 90 seconds, or until they pass the toothpick test.

Nutrition Facts Per Serving

Calories 263 Total Carbs 14g Net Carbs 12g Protein 5g Fat 20g Sugar 12g Fiber 2g

Grilled Stone Fruit

Prep time: 5 minutes, Cook time: 5 minutes, Serves: 2

Ingredients:

1 peach
1 nectarine
2 tbsps. sugar free whipped topping
What you'll need from store cupboard:
1 tbsp. Splenda
Nonstick cooking spray

Instructions:

1. Heat oven to broil. Line a shallow baking dish with foil and spray with cooking spray.
2. Cut the peach and nectarine in half and remove pits. Place cut side down in prepared dish. Broil 3 minutes.
3. Turn fruit over and sprinkle with Splenda. Broil another 2-3 minutes.
4. Transfer 1 of each fruit to a dessert bowl and top with 1 tbsp. of whipped topping. Serve.

Nutrition Facts Per Serving

Calories 101 Total Carbs 22g Net Carbs 20g Protein 1g Fat 1g Sugar 19g Fiber 2g

Fragrant Cappuccino Mousse

Prep time: 5 minutes, Chill time: 1 hour, Serves: 8

Ingredients:

2 cups low fat cream cheese, soft
1 cup nonfat half-n-half
½ cup almond milk, unsweetened
¼ cup strong brewed coffee, cooled completely
What you'll need from store cupboard:
1-2 tsps. coffee extract
1 tsp. vanilla liquid sweetener
Whole coffee beans for garnish

Instructions:

1. In a large bowl, beat cream cheese and coffee on high speed until smooth. Add milk, 1 tsp. coffee extract and liquid sweetener. Beat until smooth and thoroughly combined.
2. Pour in half-n-half and continue beating until mixture resembles the texture of mousse.
3. Spoon into dessert glasses or ramekins, cover and chill at least 1 hour before serving. Garnish with a coffee bean and serve.

Nutrition Facts Per Serving

Calories 98 Total Carbs 5g Net Carbs 3g Protein 9g Fat 5g Sugar 0g Fiber 0g

Cinnamon Chocolate Bread Pudding

Prep time: 10 minutes, Cook time: 35 minutes, Serves: 8

Ingredients:

4 cups French baguette cubes
1½ cups skim milk
3 eggs, lightly beaten
1-2 tsps. orange zest, grated
What you'll need from store cupboard:
¼ cup Splenda
¼ cup sugar-free chocolate ice cream topping
3 tbsps. unsweetened cocoa powder
1 tsp. vanilla
¾ tsp. cinnamon

Instructions:

1. Heat oven to 350°F.
2. In medium bowl, stir together Splenda and cocoa. Stir in milk, eggs, zest, vanilla, and cinnamon until well blended.
3. Place bread cubes in an 8-inch square baking dish. Pour milk mixture evenly over the top.
4. Bake 35 minutes or until a knife inserted in the center comes out clean. Cool 5-10 minutes.
5. Spoon into dessert dishes and drizzle lightly with ice cream topping. Serve.

Nutrition Facts Per Serving

Calories 139 Total Carbs 23g Net Carbs 22g Protein 6g Fat 2g Sugar 9g Fiber 1g

Coconut Carrot Cupcakes

Prep time: 10 minutes, Cook time: 35 minutes, Serves: 12

Ingredients:

2 cups carrots, grated
1 cup low fat cream cheese, soft
2 eggs
1-2 tsps. skim milk
What you'll need from store cupboard:
½ cup coconut oil, melted
¼ cup coconut flour
¼ cup Splenda
¼ tsp. stevia extract
2 tsps. vanilla, divided
1 tsp. baking powder
1 tsp. cinnamon
Nonstick cooking spray

Instructions:

1. Heat oven to 350 °F. Lightly spray a muffin pan with cooking spray, or use paper liners.
2. In a large bowl, stir together the flour, baking powder, and cinnamon.
3. Add the carrots, eggs, oil, Splenda, and vanilla to a food processor. Process until ingredients are combined but carrots still have some large chunks remaining. Add to dry ingredients and stir to combine.
4. Pour evenly into prepared pan, filling cups ⅔ full. Bake 30-35 minutes, or until cupcakes pass the toothpick test. Remove from oven and let cool.
5. In a medium bowl, beat cream cheese, stevia extract, and vanilla on high speed until smooth. Add milk, one tsp. at a time, beating after each addition, until frosting is creamy enough to spread easily.
6. Once cupcakes have cooled, spread each one with about 2 tbsps. of frosting. Chill until ready to serve.

Nutrition Facts Per Serving

Calories 160 Total Carbs 13g Net Carbs 12g Protein 4g Fat 10g Sugar 11g Fiber 1g

Coconut Cream Nut Pie

Prep time: 5 minutes, Cook time: 10 minutes, Serves: 8

Ingredients:

2 cups raw coconut, grated and divided
2 cans coconut milk, low fat and refrigerated for 24 hours
½ cup raw coconut, grated and toasted
2 tbsps. nut butter, melted
What you'll need from store cupboard:
1 cup Splenda
½ cup macadamia nuts
¼ cup almond flour

Instructions:

1. Heat oven to 350 °F.
2. Add the nuts to a food processor and pulse until finely ground. Add flour, ½ cup Splenda, and 1 cup grated coconut. Pulse until ingredients are finely ground and resemble cracker crumbs.
3. Add the nut butter and pulse until mixture starts to stick together. Press on the bottom and sides of a 9-inch pie pan. Bake 10 minutes or until golden brown. Cool
4. Turn the canned coconut upside down and open. Pour off the water and scoop the cream into a large bowl. Add remaining ½ cup Splenda and beat on high until stiff peaks form.
5. Fold in remaining 1 cup coconut and pour into crust. Cover and chill at least 2 hours. Sprinkle with toasted coconut, slice, and serve.

Nutrition Facts Per Serving

Calories 329 Total Carbs 15g Net Carbs 4g Protein 4g Fat 23g Sugar 4g Fiber 11g

Fluffy Chocolate Torte

Prep time: 15 minutes, Cook time: 35 minutes, Serves: 12

Ingredients:

5 eggs, separated, room temperature
¾ cup nut butter, sliced
What you'll need from store cupboard:
1 pkg. sugar-free chocolate chips
½ cup Splenda
¼ tsp. cream of tartar
Nonstick cooking spray

Instructions:

1. Heat oven to 350 °F. Spray a 6-7-inch springform pan with cooking spray.
2. In a microwave safe bowl, melt chocolate chips and nut butter, in 30 second intervals.
3. In a large bowl, beat egg yolks till thick and lemon colored. Beat in chocolate.
4. In a separate large bowl, with clean beaters, beat egg whites and cream of tartar till foamy. Beat in Splenda, 1 tbsp. at a time, till sugar is dissolved, continue beating till stiff glossy peaks form.
5. Fold ¼ of egg whites into chocolate mixture, then fold in the rest. Transfer to prepared pan. Bake 30-35 minutes, or center is set. Let cool completely before removing side of pan and serving.

Nutrition Facts Per Serving

Calories 181 Total Carbs 10g Net Carbs 8g Protein 3g Fat 14g Sugar 10g Fiber 0g

Cocoa Coconut Milk Shakes

Prep time: 5 minutes, blend time: 5 minutes, Serves: 2

Ingredients:

1½ cups vanilla ice cream
½ cup coconut milk, unsweetened
What you'll need from store cupboard:
2½ tbsps. coconut flakes
1 tsp. unsweetened cocoa

Instructions:

1. Heat oven to 350 °F.
2. Place coconut on a baking sheet and bake, 2-3 minutes, stirring often, until coconut is toasted.
3. Place ice cream, milk, 2 tbsps. coconut, and cocoa in a blender and process until smooth.
4. Pour into glasses and garnish with remaining toasted coconut. Serve immediately.

Nutrition Facts Per Serving

Calories 323 Total Carbs 23g Net Carbs 19g Protein 3g Fat 24g Sugar 18g Fiber 4g

German Chocolate Cake Bars

Prep time: 10 minutes, Cook time: 5 minutes, Serves: 20

Ingredients:

2 cups unsweetened coconut flakes
1 cup coconut milk, divided
¾ cup chopped pecans
¾ cup sugar-free dark baking chocolate, chopped
What you'll need from store cupboard:
1½ cups almond flour cracker crumbs
½ cup + 2 tbsps. powdered sugar substitute
½ cup coconut oil
Nonstick cooking spray

Instructions:

1. Spray an 8x8-inch baking dish with cooking spray.
2. In a large bowl, combine the coconut, ½ cup sugar substitute, cracker crumbs and pecan, stir to combine.
3. In a medium sauce pan, combine ½ cup milk and oil, cook over medium heat until oil is melted and mixture is heated through. Pour over coconut mixture and stir to combine. Press evenly in prepared baking dish and chill 1-2 hours.
4. In a clean saucepan, place the chocolate and remaining milk over med-low heat. Cook, stirring constantly, until chocolate is melted and mixture is smooth. Add the 2 tbsps. sugar substitute and stir to combine.
5. Pour chocolate over the coconut layer and chill 1 hour, or until set. Cut into squares to serve.

Nutrition Facts Per Serving

Calories 245 Total Carbs 12g Net Carbs 9g Protein 3g Fat 19g Sugar 7g Fiber 3g

Coconutty Pudding Clouds with Hazelnuts

Prep time: 5 minutes, Serves: 4

Ingredients:

2 cups low fat whipping cream
½ cup of reduced-fat cream cheese, soft
½ cup hazelnuts, ground
4 tbsps. unsweetened coconut flakes, toasted
What you'll need from store cupboard:
2 tbsps. stevia, divided
½ tsp. of vanilla
½ tsp. of hazelnut extract
½ tsp. of cacao powder, unsweetened

Instructions:

1. In a medium bowl, beat cream, vanilla, and 1 tbsp. stevia until soft peaks form.
2. In another mixing bowl, beat cream cheese, cocoa, remaining stevia, and hazelnut extract until smooth.
3. In 4 glasses, place ground nuts on the bottom, add a layer of the cream cheese mixture, then the whip cream, and top with toasted coconut. Serve immediately.

Nutrition Facts Per Serving

Calories 396 Total Carbs 12g Net Carbs 11g Protein 6g Fat 35g Sugar 9g Fiber 1g

Mini Cinnamon Bread Puddings

Prep time: 5 minutes, Cook time: 35 minutes, Serves: 12

Ingredients:

6 slices cinnamon bread, cut into cubes
1¼ cups skim milk
½ cup egg substitute
1 tbsp. nut butter, melted
What you'll need from store cupboard:
⅓ cup Splenda
1 tsp. vanilla
⅛ tsp. salt
⅛ tsp. nutmeg

Instructions:

1. Heat oven to 350°F. Line 12 medium-size muffin cups with paper baking cups.
2. In a large bowl, stir together milk, egg substitute, Splenda, vanilla, salt and nutmeg until combined. Add bread cubes and stir until moistened. Let rest 15 minutes.
3. Spoon evenly into prepared baking cups. Drizzle nut butter evenly over the tops. Bake 30-35 minutes or until puffed and golden brown. Remove from oven and let cool completely.

Nutrition Facts Per Serving

Calories 105 Total Carbs 16 Net Carbs 15g Protein 4g Fat 2g Sugar 9g Fiber 1g

Lemon Meringue Coconut Ice Cream

Prep time: 5 minutes, Cook time: 15 minutes, Serves: 8

Ingredients:

4 eggs, separated
2 cans coconut milk, refrigerated for 24 hours
6 tbsps. fresh lemon juice
Zest of 2 lemons
What you'll need from store cupboard:
2½ tbsps. liquid stevia
1 tbsp. vanilla
1 tsp. cream of tartar

Instructions:

1. Heat oven to 325 °F.
2. In a medium bowl, beat the egg whites and cream of tartar on high speed until soft peaks from. Add 1½ tbsps. of stevia and continue beating on high until stiff peaks from.
3. Spread the meringue in a small baking dish and bake 15 minutes, or until the top is golden brown. Remove from oven and let cool completely.
4. Turn the canned coconut milk upside down and open. Drain off the water, save it for another use later. Scoop the cream into a large bowl. Add the egg yolks, juice, zest, remaining tbsp. of stevia, and vanilla and beat until ingredients are thoroughly combined.
5. Pour into an ice cream maker and freeze according to directions.
6. In a liter sized plastic container, spread a layer of ice cream to cover the bottom. Top with a layer of meringue. Repeat layers. Place an airtight cover on the container and freeze at least 3 hours before serving.

Nutrition Facts Per Serving

Calories 152 Total Carbs 3g Net Carbs 1g Protein 4g Fat 14g Sugar 1g Fiber 0g

No Bake Lemon Coconut Tart

Prep time: 10 minutes, Chill time: 2 hours, Serves: 8

Ingredients:

½ cup nut butter, soft
⅓ cup + 3 tbsps. fresh lemon juice, divided
⅓ cup almond milk, unsweetened
4½ tbsps. nut butter, melted
3-4 tbsps. lemon zest, grated fine
What you'll need from store cupboard:
1 cup almond flour
¾ cup coconut, grated fine
¼ cup + 3 tbsps. Splenda
2½ tsps. vanilla, divided
2 tsps. lemon extract
¼ tsp. salt

Instructions:

1. Spray a 9-inch tart pan with cooking spray.
2. In a medium bowl combine, flour, coconut, 3 tbsps. lemon juice, 2 tbsps. Splenda, melted nut butter, 1½ tsps. vanilla, and a pinch of salt until thoroughly combined. Dump into prepared pan and press evenly on bottom and halfway up sides. Cover and chill until ready to use.
3. In a medium bowl, beat the soft nut butter until fluffy. Add remaining ingredients and beat until mixture is smooth. Taste and add more lemon juice or Splenda if desired.
4. Pour the filling into the crust. Cover and chill until filling is set, about 2 hours.

Nutrition Facts Per Serving

Calories 317 Total Carbs 17g Net Carbs 15g Protein 3g Fat 25g Sugar 13g Fiber 2g

Lemon Peach Ice Cream

Prep time: 15 minutes, Chill time: 4 hours, Serves: 32

Ingredients:

4 peaches, peel and chop
8 oz. fat free whipped topping
2 cups skim milk
¼ cup fresh lemon juice
What you'll need from store cupboard:
2 (12 oz.) cans fat free evaporated milk
14 oz. can unsweetened condensed milk
3.4 oz. pkg. sugar free instant vanilla pudding mix
½ cup Splenda
1 tsp. vanilla
½ tsp. almond extract
⅛ tsp. salt

Instructions:

1. In a large bowl, beat milk and pudding mix on low speed 2 minutes. Beat in remaining ingredients, except whipped topping until thoroughly combined. Fold in whipped topping.
2. Freeze in ice cream maker according to manufacturer's directions, this may take 2 batches. Transfer to freezer containers and freeze 4 hours before serving. Serving size is ½ cup.

Nutrition Facts Per Serving

Calories 106 Total Carbs 19g Net Carbs 15g Protein 3g Fat 1g Sugar 15g Fiber 0g

Frozen Pineapple Yogurt

Prep time: 5 minutes, Chill time: 1 hour, Serves: 4

Ingredients:

½ cup half-and-half
½ cup plain reduced-fat yogurt
¼ cup egg substitute
What you'll need from store cupboard:
¾ cup crushed pineapple, in juice
¼ cup Splenda

Instructions:

1. In a medium bowl, beat egg substitute until thick and cream colored. Add remaining ingredients and mix to thoroughly combine. Cover and chill completely, if using an ice cream maker. Once chilled add to ice cream maker and freeze according to manufacturer's directions.
2. Or, you can pour the mixture into a shallow glass baking dish and freeze. Stir and scrape the mixture, every 10 minutes, with a rubber spatula until it reaches desired consistency, about 1 hour.

Nutrition Facts Per Serving

Calories 145 Total Carbs 20g Net Carbs 17g Protein 5g Fat 4g Sugar 17g Fiber 0g

Cranberry Watermelon Ice

Prep time: 5 minutes, Chill time: 8 hours, Serves: 8

Ingredients:

5 cups cubed watermelon, remove seeds
½ cup light cranberry juice cocktail
What you'll need from store cupboard:
½ cup Splenda
1 envelope unflavored gelatin

Instructions:

1. Place watermelon in a food processor and pulse until almost smooth.
2. In a small saucepan, over low heat, stir together Splenda and gelatin. Slowly add juice. Cook, stirring, until gelatin dissolves.
3. Add to watermelon and process until combined.
4. Pour into an 8-inch square dish, cover and freeze 5 hours, or until firm.
5. Break watermelon mixture into chunks. Freeze another 3 hours.
6. To serve: scrape and stir mixture with a fork to create an icy texture. Spoon into dessert dishes and serve.

Nutrition Facts Per Serving

Calories 94 Total Carbs 20g Net Carbs 16g Protein 1g Fat 0g Sugar 18g Fiber 0g

Apple Cider Vinaigrette, page 70

Asian Hot Mustard, page 70

Basic BBQ Sauce, page 70

Dijon Citrus Vinaigrette, page 70

Chapter 13 Sauces, Dips & Dressings Recipe

Apple Cider Vinaigrette

Total time: 5 minutes, Serves: 8

Ingredients:

What you'll need from store cupboard:
½ cup sunflower oil
¼ cup apple cider vinegar
¼ cup apple juice, unsweetened
¼ tsp. stevia extract
1 tbsp. lemon juice
½ tsp. salt
Freshly ground black pepper, to taste

Instructions:

1. Place all ingredients in a mason jar. Screw on lid and shake until everything is thoroughly combined. Store in refrigerator until ready to use. Shake well before using.

Nutrition Facts Per Serving

Calories 138 Total Carbs 4g Net Carbs 2g Protein 0g Fat 13g Sugar 4g Fiber 0g

Basic BBQ Sauce

Prep time: 5 minutes, Cook time: 20 minutes, Serves: 20

Ingredients:

What you'll need from store cupboard:
2½ (6 oz.) cans tomato paste
1½ cups water
½ cup apple cider vinegar
⅓ cup swerve confectioners
2 tbsps. Worcestershire sauce
1 tbsp. liquid hickory smoke
2 tsps. smoked paprika
1 tsp. garlic powder
½ tsp. onion powder
½ tsp. salt
¼ tsp. chili powder
¼ tsp. cayenne pepper

Instructions:

1. Whisk all ingredients, but water, together in a saucepan. Add water, starting with 1 cup, whisking it in, until mixture resembles a thin barbecue sauce.
2. Bring to a low boil over med-high heat. Reduce heat to med-low and simmer, stirring frequently, 20 minutes, or sauce has thickened slightly.
3. Taste and adjust seasoning until you like it. Cool completely. Store in a jar with an airtight lid in the refrigerator. Serving size is 2 tbsps. of sauce.

Nutrition Facts Per Serving

Calories 24 Total Carbs 9g Net Carbs 8g Protein 1g Fat 0g Sugar 7g Fiber 1g

Asian Hot Mustard

Prep time: 15 minutes, Total time: 15 minutes, Serves: 4

Ingredients:

What you'll need from store cupboard:
1 tbsp. mustard powder
1½ tsps. hot water
½ tsp. vegetable oil
½ tsp. rice vinegar
⅛ tsp. salt
⅛ tsp. white pepper

Instructions:

1. In a small bowl, mix together the dry ingredients. Add water and stir until mixture resembles liquid paste and dry ingredients are absorbed.
2. Stir in oil and vinegar until thoroughly combined. Cover and let rest 10 minutes.
3. Stir again. Taste and adjust any seasonings if desired. Cover and refrigerate until ready to use.

Nutrition Facts Per Serving

Calories 19 Total Carbs 1g Net Carbs 0g Protein 1g Fat 1g Sugar 0g Fiber 0g

Dijon Citrus Vinaigrette

Prep time: 5 minutes, Total time: 10 minutes, Serves: 6

Ingredients:

1 orange, zested and juiced
1 lemon, zested and juiced
What you'll need from store cupboard:
¼ cup extra virgin olive oil
1 tsp. Dijon mustard
¼ tsp. stevia
1 clove garlic, crushed
Salt & pepper, to taste

Instructions:

1. Place the zest and juices, mustard, stevia, garlic, salt and pepper in a food processor. Pulse to combine.
2. With the machine running, slowly pour in the olive oil and process until combined.
3. Use right away, or store in a jar with an airtight lid in the refrigerator.

Nutrition Facts Per Serving

Calories 94 Total Carbs 6g Net Carbs 5g Protein 0g Fat 8g Sugar 4g Fiber 1g

Orange Blueberry Dessert Sauce

Prep time: 5 minutes, Cook time: 10 minutes, Serves: 16

Ingredients:

1½ cups orange segments
1 cup blueberries
¼ cup orange juice
What you'll need from store cupboard:
¼ cup water
⅓ cup almonds, sliced
3 tbsps. Splenda
1 tbsp. cornstarch
⅛ tsp. salt

Instructions:

1. In a small saucepan, combine Splenda, cornstarch, and salt. Whisk in orange juice and water until smooth.
2. Bring to a boil over med-high heat, cook, stirring frequently, 1-2 minutes or until thickened.
3. Reduce heat and stir in fruit. Cook 5 minutes. Remove from heat and let cool completely.
4. Store in an airtight jar in the refrigerator until ready to use. Serving size is 1 tablespoon.

Nutrition Facts Per Serving

Calories 46 Total Carbs 8g Net Carbs 6g Protein 1g Fat 1g Sugar 6g Fiber 0g

Italian-Style Salsa

Prep time: 10 minutes, Chill time: 1 hour, Serves: 16

Ingredients:

4 plum tomatoes, diced
½ red onion, diced fine
2 tbsps. fresh parsley, diced
What you'll need from store cupboard:
12 Kalamata olives, pitted and chopped
2 cloves garlic, diced fine
1 tbsp. balsamic vinegar
1 tbsp. olive oil
2 tsps. capers, drained
¼ tsp. salt
¼ tsp. pepper

Instructions:

1. In a medium bowl, combine all ingredients and stir to mix. Cover and chill 1 hour before using.
2. Store in a jar with an airtight lid in the refrigerator up to 7 days. Stir before using.

Nutrition Facts Per Serving

Calories 21 Total Carbs 2g Net Carbs 1g Protein 0g Fat 1g Sugar 1g Fiber 0g

Easy Pizza Sauce

Prep time: 5 minutes, Cook time: 5 minutes, Serves: 8

Ingredients:

½ cup yellow onion, diced
What you'll need from store cupboard:
15 oz. tomatoes, crushed, no sugar added
⅓ cup + 1 tbsp. olive oil
3 cloves garlic, diced
2 tsps. parsley
1 tsp. rosemary
1 tsp. thyme
1 tsp. smoked paprika
Salt, to taste

Instructions:

1. Heat 1 tbsp. oil in a small skillet over medium heat. Add onion and garlic and cook until onions are translucent.
2. In a medium saucepan, over medium heat, stir all ingredients together, along with onions. Bring to a simmer and cook 2-3 minutes, stirring constantly.
3. Remove from heat and let cool completely. Store in a jar with an air tight lid in the refrigerator up to 2 weeks. Or in the freezer up to 6 months.

Nutrition Facts Per Serving

Calories 179 Total Carbs 8g Net carbs 6g Protein 2g Fat 17g Sugar 5g Fiber 2g

Queso Verde Salsa

Prep time: 10 minutes, Cook time: 30 minutes, Serves: 10

Ingredients:

½ package cream cheese, soft
½ cup white American cheese, cubed
½ cup white cheddar cheese, cubed
½ cup pepper Jack cheese, cubed
¼ cup skim milk
What you'll need from store cupboard:
½ cup salsa verde
½ cup green chilies, diced
Nonstick cooking spray

Instructions:

1. Heat oven to 325 °F. Spray a small baking dish with cooking spray.
2. In a medium mixing bowl, combine all ingredients. Add to prepared baking dish.
3. Bake 30 minutes, stirring every 8-10 minutes, until cheese is melted and dip is hot and bubbly. Serve warm.

Nutrition Facts Per Serving

Calories 105 Total Carbs 3g Net Carbs 2g Protein 7g Fat 7g Sugar 1g Fiber 1g

Homemade Marinara Sauce

Prep time: 10 minutes, Cook time: 30 minutes, Serves: 6

Ingredients:
What you'll need from store cupboard:
28 oz. can diced tomatoes, undrained
4-6 cloves garlic, diced fine
4 tbsps. extra virgin olive oil
2 tbsps. tomato paste
1 tbsp. basil
1 tsp. Splenda
1 tsp. salt

Instructions:
1. Heat oil in saucepan over medium heat. Add the garlic and cook 1 minute.
2. Stir in the tomato paste and cook 1 minute more. Add the tomatoes and basil and simmer 10-15 minutes, breaking up the tomatoes as they cook.
3. Stir in Splenda and salt. Use an immersion blender and process to desired consistency.
4. Let cool and store in a jar with an airtight lid in the refrigerator up to 7 days. Or use right away.

Nutrition Facts Per Serving

Calories 179 Total Carbs 13g Net Carbs 10g Protein 2g Fat 14g Sugar 8g Fiber 3g

Sugar Free Ketchup

Prep time: 5 minutes, Total time: 5 minutes, Serves: 28

Ingredients:
What you'll need from store cupboard:
12 oz. tomato paste
1½ cups water
⅓ cup white vinegar
1 tbsp. salt
3 tsps. Splenda
1 tsp. onion powder

Instructions:
1. In a large bowl, combine water, vinegar, Splenda, onion powder, and salt. Whisk in tomato paste until smooth.
2. Pour into a glass jar with an air tight lid and store in refrigerator until ready to use. Serving size is 2 tablespoons.

Nutrition Facts Per Serving

Calories 15 Total Carbs 3g Net Carbs 1g Protein 0g Fat 0g Sugar 2g Fiber 0g

Sriracha Mayo Dipping Sauce

Prep time: 1 minute, Total time: 2 minutes, Serves: 6

Ingredients:
2 tsps. fresh lime juice
What you'll need from store cupboard:
½ cup lite mayonnaise
2 tbsps. Sriracha sauce
1 tbsp. Splenda
1 tsp. Worcestershire sauce

Instructions:
1. In a small bowl, stir all the ingredients together until smooth.
2. Use right away, or cover and refrigerate until ready to use. Serving size is 1½ tablespoons.

Nutrition Facts Per Serving

Calories 83 Total Carbs 5g Net Carbs 3g Protein 0g Fat 7g Sugar 2g Fiber 0g

Roasted Tomato Salsa

Prep time: 10 minutes, Cook time: 30 minutes, Serves: 8

Ingredients:
6 plum tomatoes
1¼ cups cilantro
What you'll need from store cupboard:
2 tsps. olive oil
1 tsp. adobo sauce
½ tsp. salt, divided
Nonstick cooking spray

Instructions:
1. Heat oven to 425 °F. Spray a broiler pan with cooking spray.
2. Cut tomatoes in half and remove seeds. Place, cut side up, on broiler pan. Brush with oil and sprinkle with ¼ tsp. salt. Turn tomatoes cut side down and bake 30-40 minutes or until edges are browned.
3. Place cilantro in food processor and pulse until coarsely chopped. Add tomatoes, adobo, and remaining salt. Process until chunky. Store in jar with air tight lid and refrigerate until ready to use. Serving size is 2 tablespoons.

Nutrition Facts Per Serving

Calories 33 Total Carbs 5g Net Carbs 4g Protein 1g Fat 1g Sugar 4g Fiber 1g

Tangy Mexican Salad dressing

Total time: 5 minutes, Serves: 8

Ingredients:
½ cup cilantro, diced fine
3 tbsps. fresh lime juice
What you'll need from store cupboard:
½ cup sunflower oil
2 tbsps. water
1 tbsp. apple cider vinegar
¼ tsp. stevia
1 tsp. garlic salt
½ tsp. Mexican oregano
Freshly ground black pepper, to taste

Instructions:
1. Add all ingredients to a food processor or blender. Pulse until well blended and emulsified. Taste and adjust seasonings as desired.
2. Store in an air-tight container in the refrigerator. To serve, bring to room temperature and shake well.

Nutrition Facts Per Serving

Calories 127 Total Carbs 2g Net Carbs 1g Protein 0 Fat 14g Sugar 2g Fiber 0g

Dijon Walnut Vinaigrette

Total time: 5 minutes, Serves: 4

Ingredients:
What you'll need from store cupboard:
½ cup water
¼ cup balsamic vinegar
¼ cup walnuts
¼ cup raisins
1 clove garlic
1 tsp. Dijon mustard
¼ tsp. thyme

Instructions:
1. Place all ingredients in a blender or food processor and pulse until smooth. Store in a jar with an air tight lid in the refrigerator.

Nutrition Facts Per Serving

Calories 53 Total Carbs 2g Net Carbs 1g Protein 2g Fat 5g Sugar 0g Fiber 1g

Maple Mustard Dressing

Total time: 5 minutes, Serves: 6

Ingredients:
What you'll need from store cupboard:
2 tbsps. balsamic vinegar
2 tbsps. olive oil
1 tbsp. sugar free maple syrup
1 tsp. Dijon mustard
⅛ tsp. sea salt

Instructions:
1. Place all the ingredients in a jar with a tight fitting lid. Screw on lid and shake to combine. Store in refrigerator until ready to use.

Nutrition Facts Per Serving

Calories 48 Total Carbs 2g Net Carbs 1g Protein 0g Fat 5g Sugar 0g Fiber 0g

Maple Shallot Vinaigrette

Prep time: 3 minutes, Total time: 5 minutes, Serves: 4

Ingredients:
1 tbsp. shallot, diced fine
What you'll need from store cupboard:
2 tbsps. apple cider vinegar
1 tbsp. spicy brown mustard
1 tbsp. olive oil
2 tsps. sugar free maple syrup

Instructions:
1. Place all ingredients in a small jar with an airtight lid. Shake well to mix. Refrigerate until ready to use. Serving size is 1 tablespoon.

Nutrition Facts Per Serving

Calories 45 Total Carbs 5g Net Carbs 3g Protein 0g Fat 2g Sugar 0g Fiber 0g

Appendix 1: Measurement Conversion Chart

Volume Equivalents (Dry)

US STANDARD	METRIC (APPROXIMATE)
1/8 teaspoon	0.5 mL
1/4 teaspoon	1 mL
1/2 teaspoon	2 mL
3/4 teaspoon	4 mL
1 teaspoon	5 mL
1 tablespoon	15 mL
1/4 cup	59 mL
1/2 cup	118 mL
3/4 cup	177 mL
1 cup	235 mL
2 cups	475 mL
3 cups	700 mL
4 cups	1 L

Temperatures Equivalents

FAHRENHEIT (F)	CELSIUS(C) (APPROXIMATE)
225 °F	107 °C
250 °F	120 °C
275 °F	135 °C
300 °F	150 °C
325 °F	160 °C
350 °F	180 °C
375 °F	190 °C
400 °F	205 °C
425 °F	220 °C
450 °F	235 °C
475 °F	245 °C
500 °F	260 °C

Volume Equivalents (Liquid)

US STANDARD	US STANDARD (OUNCES)	METRIC (APPROXIMATE)
2 tablespoons	1 fl.oz.	30 mL
1/4 cup	2 fl.oz.	60 mL
1/2 cup	4 fl.oz.	120 mL
1 cup	8 fl.oz.	240 mL
1 1/2 cup	12 fl.oz.	355 mL
2 cups or 1 pint	16 fl.oz.	475 mL
4 cups or 1 quart	32 fl.oz.	1 L
1 gallon	128 fl.oz.	4 L

Weight Equivalents

US STANDARD	METRIC (APPROXIMATE)
1 ounce	28 g
2 ounces	57 g
5 ounces	142 g
10 ounces	284 g
15 ounces	425 g
16 ounces (1 pound)	455 g
1.5 pounds	680 g
2 pounds	907 g

Appendix 2: The Dirty Dozen and Clean Fifteen

The Environmental Working Group (EWG) is a widely known organization that has an eminent guide to pesticides and produce. More specifically, the group takes in data from tests conducted by the US Department of Agriculture (USDA) and then categorizes produce into a list titled "Dirty Dozen," which ranks the twelve top produce items that contain the most pesticide residues, or alternatively the "Clean Fifteen," which ranks fifteen produce items that are contaminated with the least amount of pesticide residues.

The EWG has recently released their 2021 Dirty Dozen list, and this year strawberries, spinach and kale – with a few other produces which will be revealed shortly – are listed at the top of the list. This year's ranking is similar to the 2020 Dirty Dozen list, with the few differences being that collards and mustard greens have joined kale at number three on the list. Other changes include peaches and cherries, which having been listed subsequently as seventh and eighth on the 2020 list, have now been flipped; the introduction – which the EWG has said is the first time ever – of bell and hot peppers into the 2021 list; and the departure of potatoes from the twelfth spot.

DIRTY DOZEN LIST

Strawberries	Apples	Pears
Spinach	Grapes	Bell and hot peppers
Kale, collards and mustard greens	Cherries	Celery
Nectarines	Peaches	Tomatoes

CLEAN FIFTEEN LIST

Avocados	Sweet peas (frozen)	Kiwi
Sweet corn	Eggplant	Cauliflower
Pineapple	Asparagus	Mushrooms
Onions	Broccoli	Honeydew melon
Papaya	Cabbage	Cantaloupe

These lists are created to help keep the public informed on their potential exposures to pesticides, which then allows for better and healthier food choices to be made.

This is the advice that ASEQ-EHAQ also recommends. Stay clear of the dirty dozen by opting for their organic versions, and always be mindful of what you are eating and how it was grown. Try to eat organic as much as possible – whether it is on the list, or not.

Appendix 3: Recipes Index

Made in the USA
Las Vegas, NV
17 September 2023

77722299R00050